MANAGING VULNERABILITY

Studies in Rhetoric/Communication
Thomas W. Benson, Series Editor

MANAGING VULNERABILITY

South Africa's Struggle for a Democratic Rhetoric

Richard C. Marback

The University of South Carolina Press

Published by the University of South Carolina Press
Columbia, South Carolina 29208

www.sc.edu/uscpress

Manufactured in the United States of America

21 20 19 18 17 16 15 14 13 12   10 9 8 7 6 5 4 3 2 1

Library of Congress Cataloging-in-Publication Data

Marback, Richard.
  Managing vulnerability : South Africa's struggle for a democratic
rhetoric / Richard C. Marback.
      p. cm.— (Studies in rhetoric/communication)
  Includes bibliographical references and index.
  ISBN 978-1-61117-099-3 (hardback : alk. paper)
    1. Rhetoric—Political aspects—South Africa. 2. Expression—Political aspects—
South Africa. 3. Democratization—South Africa. 4. Reconciliation. 5. Post-apartheid
era—South Africa. 6. Sobukwe, Robert Mangaliso—Political and social views.
7. Mandela, Nelson, 1918—Political and social views. I. Title. II. Series: Studies in
rhetoric/communication.
    JA85.2.S63M37 2012
      808.50968—DC23   2012019779

CONTENTS

SERIES EDITOR'S PREFACE

In *Managing Vulnerability: South Africa's Struggle for a Democratic Rhetoric,* Richard C. Marback argues that in the struggle for South African freedom, democracy, and reconciliation, the reciprocal questions of vulnerability and sovereignty of the people and groups engaged in the long struggle shapes the rhetoric and response of all participants. Marback acknowledges the affirmative force of claims by scholars such as Eric Doxtader and Philippe-Joseph Salazar that the mostly peaceful South African transition from apartheid to democracy—entailing rhetorical occasions of inclusive deliberation and reconciliation—demonstrates the efficacy of rhetoric and the potential of South African democracy. At the same time, Marback acknowledges the competing claim that Western rhetoric may be an alien importation to the South African scene, as well as the objection that while the democratic transition may have witnessed widespread participation and inclusion, material injustices remain.

In a series of case studies, Marback explores how the natural human impulse to guard ourselves from material or emotional vulnerability, aspiring to a personal, and perhaps rhetorical, sovereignty, makes it harder for us and others to appeal and attend to each other honestly, since one person's sovereignty may seem another person's vulnerability. The South African freedom struggle found ways to transcend the raw divisions created by the Afrikaner "ambitions for invulnerability." In doing so the freedom movement moved beyond simply challenging the language of Afrikaner invulnerable sovereignty through a struggle "to give expression to . . . sovereign vulnerability—a capacity for rhetorical agency grounded in openness to the anger and antagonism, frailty and suffering, hope and joy of others." The model for such shared, sovereign vulnerability that Marback finds especially in Robert Sobukwe, Nelson Mandela, and Desmond Tutu is not, Marback argues, guaranteed, though he sees prospects for hope of a rhetoric of common good in the face of ongoing challenges of HIV/AIDS, poverty, violence, and other legacies of the apartheid regime.

Professor Marback offers the hope that the critical vocabulary of vulnerability and sovereignty that he finds in South African rhetoric may offer tools for meeting the challenges of the South African experience.

THOMAS W. BENSON

Chapter 1

THE PROMISE OF PARTICIPATION

The transition from apartheid to democracy in South Africa affirms for many the wealth of resources available in rhetoric that make it possible for people to overcome temptations to solve their problems through violence. The negotiated settlement leading to democratic elections and the public performance of reconciliation promoting the spread of democracy have been seen as renewing in us what Erik Doxtader has described as our faith in the possibilities of words shared with each other. Among scholars who celebrate the transition from apartheid Philippe-Joseph Salazar has been one of the most prominent advocates for appealing to rhetoric to make sense of—and further promote—the emergence of South African democracy. He argues emphatically for embracing the necessity of institutional negotiation and public deliberation as the "sovereign duty" of democratic citizens, the duty to contribute to a "contest of words about competing truths" ("Truth in Politics," 14). Salazar's appeal to rhetoric as a citizen's sovereign duty invokes the responsibility to, as well as the potential for authority in, acts of public deliberation that give meaning and purpose to lives lived together. The appeal is familiar enough. People who act as citizens, who can and do submit their expressions to a public forum of competing truths, take part in discussions meant to make a more meaningful life available to all. Invoking Hannah Arendt, Salazar explains the nature of the democratic "contest of words" as a forum in which citizens express views they hold to be true while listening in earnest to the views expressed by others, all the while expecting from their fellow citizens the same forthrightness and regard. This act of publicly expressing individual views forms a democracy through aggregation, the "transient, fragmented, often-community-based" truth of "prejudice, opinion, belief, perception" (13). Far from cynically portraying public truth as nothing more than the fickle assertions of custom and preference, Salazar's characterization of South African public rhetoric celebrates and encourages the open-endedness of the project of people living together as citizens who are figuring out for themselves the course of their shared lives instead of having that course charted for them.

Salazar points to the public testimonies given before the South African Truth and Reconciliation Commission (TRC) as evidence of the virtue and necessity of citizen rhetoric in the narration of South African nationhood, the "telling of stories" that makes available to everyone a source of meaning that no one person can have in isolation ("Truth in Politics," 16). He makes his point about the need for inclusiveness most clearly near the end of *An African Athens* when he writes, "South African society is nurturing a political model for integrating differences within social deliberation. This has a name in the tradition of democratic thought: It is called the common good" (165). There can be no doubt Salazar is right about participation marking the transition from apartheid to democracy. The four days from April 26 to 29 in 1994 when South Africans stood in line for hours to vote in their first democratic election provided a poignant image of the strength in the people of a desire to participate. And the tale told by Antjie Krog in *Country of My Skull* of those ordinary people who appealed for amnesty to the TRC because they felt they had not done enough to end apartheid speaks less to a sense of guilt and more to a feeling of wanting to do more to contribute to nurturing a common good. As Krog so aptly put it, the TRC gave birth to South Africa's language itself (42), a language of the common good that encourages everyone's participation.

People who have faith in the power of words—people like Doxtader, Salazar, and Krog—would seem to have every reason to be enthusiastic about the prospects of South Africans using language to shape democratic South Africa. But not everyone has that faith and shares that enthusiasm. James L. Gibson, for one, remarks, "based on my casual observations of the South African media, complaints and condemnations of the truth and reconciliation process seem to far outnumber laudatory assessments" (*Overcoming Apartheid*, 2). John Dugard cautions that the project of reconciliation "minimizes the memory of apartheid" (284). Graeme Simpson further warns that "there is a real possibility that the TRC, by granting amnesty to confessed killers, may actually have contributed to the sense of impunity that feeds the burgeoning rate of violent crime" (247). Additional criticisms are not hard to find, and they do not vary much in their negative assessments of the TRC. What these criticisms share is the concern, expressed by Gibson, Dugard, and Graeme, that the language of forgiveness and reconciliation by itself does little to provide any justice. What Gibson, Dugard, Graeme, and countless others argue is that the public discourse of the TRC failed because it was primarily a display of words, nothing more than empty rhetoric, a public performance of reconciliation that did little more than distract people's attention from the government's failure to redress basic social inequalities.

Critics of the TRC have legitimate concerns. Apartheid-era disenfranchisement continues to leave black South Africans disproportionately vulnerable to disease, homelessness, hunger, joblessness, poverty, and violence. Without denying systemic inequality and injustice, I believe it would be the height of cynicism to say enthusiastic responses to the TRC—as well as to the democratic transition in South Africa—give expression to nothing more than a kind of naïveté. More is at stake in disagreements about South Africa's democratic progress than a choice between liberal optimism and socialist skepticism. What divides the critics from the apologists is their disagreement over the relationship of sovereign-citizen participation to conditions that create and perpetuate vulnerability. For the critics talk of a common good, of participation, and of reconciliation does nothing to redress the material inequalities and physical hardships that diminish the life chances of so many South Africans. For apologists participation in talk about a common good is an essential part of the ongoing process of redressing inequality and injustice.

My concern here in drawing attention to the divide in responses to the TRC is to focus on points of convergence. Where apologists and critics converge is in their mutual interest in the consequences hardship and participation can and do have on each other. The persistence of these convergent issues—issues regarding the capacity in uses of language to contribute (or not) to real social progress, not only to negotiation, reconciliation, and agreement about a common good, but also to alleviation of the suffering caused by material inequality —have certainly tempered enthusiasm for aspirations to democracy in South Africa. At the same time, though, I think continued debate regarding these issues suggests there is still room to be hopeful about democratic progress. Of course the possibility for hope must realistically face the challenges of the situation. To be both hopeful and realistic requires of us that we consider questions about what it involves and what it means for citizens to participate in defining a common good. Questions about the conditions necessary and sufficient for widespread participation are primarily though not exclusively questions about how much and in what ways increased susceptibility to the ravages of material inequality decreases effective participation in a democracy. These are questions that have at their core definitions of both sovereignty and vulnerability, definitions which in turn have significant impact on understandings of not only the notion of a common good but also of the conditions both necessary and sufficient for democratic participation in the making of that common good. *Managing Vulnerability* offers insight into these questions. My view is that the opposition of rhetorical sovereignty to material vulnerability lies at the center of the disagreement between apologists and critics of South African democracy, and I argue that sovereignty and vulnerability are not easily—or always usefully—disentangled.

We get most directly to issues regarding ambivalence about the role played by public expressions of forgiveness and reconciliation in the transition to democracy in South Africa by considering enthusiasm for rhetoric in the nurturing of a common good. It is for this reason that Salazar's work on rhetoric in the country is a productive starting point. Salazar characterizes a citizen's sovereign duty as one of rhetorical contestation and competition, and he describes the common good resulting from the collective exercise of sovereign duty as an ongoing aggregation of difference that only enriches our understandings of ourselves and our interactions with others. Already we can sense problems. Experience tells us that this characterization expresses more of an ambition than a reality, that this is at best an overly generous description of what it is to develop a sense of the common good out of deliberations about differences. Deliberation is by definition an activity of having to make a choice among available options regarding an issue of broad concern typically involving the allocation or use of limited resources, as when the people of South Africa must decide the issue of land reparation for those who were forcibly removed from their homes during apartheid. Questions regarding the need for and nature of land reparations are in themselves difficult enough. The availability of limited funds makes questions of distributing reparations that much more difficult to decide, while deciding procedures for who may qualify for the limited resources further burdens deliberations with the prospect of failed compromise. Salazar does not deny this. At the same time his argument does suggest there are in democratic deliberation no losers. Salazar's hope for a positive experience for all emerges through his emphasis on the collective experience of deliberation and democracy as something in which every expression is as valuable and valued as every other because all contribute to a collective groping toward the common good. However much we may want this to be true, experience tells us that people engaged in deliberating over important issues do not always feel themselves valued even if their participation does in the end contribute to the greater good of all.

If we want to hold on to deliberation as a vital discourse of democracy we need a richer characterization of the experience of participation than Salazar

seems to provide. We need this characterization so that we might be better able
to convince those who experience the sting of having been chosen against that
they and their contributions do matter. Amy Gutmann and Dennis Thompson have attempted to provide just such a rich characterization in *Democracy
and Disagreement,* where they argue from the example of the United States that
deliberation is vital to the health and well being of any democracy. They conclude we must deliberate with each other if we are to productively manage the
disagreements and dissatisfactions that follow from the "scarcity, limited generosity, incompatible values, and incomplete understanding" defining our lives
together (347). Gutmann and Thompson do not suggest that deliberation elim-
inates disagreement or that it promises the end of dissatisfaction. Instead the
conditions providing for democratic deliberation—reciprocity, publicity, and
accountability—hold out the best hope for what Gutmann and Thompson call
the "quest for reasonable terms of social cooperation" (353). Social cooperation
does not just happen. For deliberation to be effectively democratic Gutmann
and Thompson recognize the need for institutions both to educate citizens in
deliberating and to structure their opportunities for participating. Institutions
that make it possible for citizens to deliberate democratically not only provide
access to opportunities, they also prepare citizens to give reasons others can
accept for consequences all will have to share. This does not take the sting out
of any one decision, such as the decision to grant reparations to this person and
not to that person. At best adequate institutional provision for democratic participation makes it possible for citizens to look forward to other deliberations
and to anticipate different outcomes from future deliberations.

  This way of looking at the problem sketches in an answer to critics who say
that the measure of democracy's failure in South Africa is the extent to which
it has not yet addressed inequality. Filling in the answer to the critics would
involve following Gutmann and Thompson by saying that current disappointment with the rate of social progress should not lead us to discount prospects
for future progress. We need to take seriously people's discontent and provide
them reassurances that everything is being done to make as much progress as
possible. Critics might answer that this kind of forestalling of disappointment
is precisely the problem, that participation in deliberation about land restitution in South Africa gives people just enough hope to make them complacent
but not quite enough resources to make their lives better. To this supporters of
deliberation can answer that talk about disappointment and the pace of progress
are important to the success of any and all deliberations. Supporters can follow
this claim by further arguing that the very fact that citizens are participating in
deliberation is itself a good not to be discounted. We can continue in this way

and linger unproductively at this impasse if we do not draw more critically from debate over Gutmann and Thompson's conception of democratic deliberation.

Their description of democratic deliberation is comprehensive, but it is not without its critics. Responses to Gutmann and Thompson pointing out the shortcomings of their view have focused on two themes. First is the overemphasis on deliberation as the discourse central to democracy. Jane Mansbridge for one has argued for the importance of what she terms "everyday talk" to the public life of a democracy, talk which sustains relationships as well as values. Michael Walzer also enlarges the list of discursive activities vital to a democracy. Without discounting the importance of deliberation he places it alongside other non-deliberative discursive activities—including mobilizing, demonstrating, fund-raising, and campaigning—all of which give expression to the political values of "passion, commitment, solidarity, courage, and competitiveness (59), values which he argues are as important to the expression of democracy as the values of reciprocity, publicity, and accountability that ground deliberation.

The second thread of criticism focuses on the problem of inclusion in democratic deliberations. As Iris Marion Young makes clear, inclusion in delib-erations is not only a practical problem for large-scale democracies, inclusion is at the same time a principle that ought to define the terms for democratic deliberations. According to Young democracies need to do more than prohibit exclusion. For deliberations to be truly democratic, democratic institutions need to promote inclusion by concerning themselves with "the timing, location, and structure of deliberative events." One way they can do this is by encourag-ing "relatively unorganized constituencies to organize themselves," while at the same time curtailing the disproportionate participation of constituencies with greater access ("Justice" 156).

As important as greater access for all is to a democracy, issues of inclusion turn on more than crafting an equality of opportunities for participating in deliberations. Elsewhere Young develops her critique of deliberation by arguing more fully against the "culturally biased conception of [deliberative] discus-sion that tends to silence or devalue some people or groups" less familiar with and less capable of that kind of discursive decision-making ("Communication" 60). She proposes redressing the exclusivity of democratic deliberation with a notion of "communicative democracy" that begins with understanding "differ-ences of culture, social perspective, or particularist commitment as resources to draw on . . . rather than as divisions to be overcome" (60). Less important here is the ambition to discern some common good that all agree to. More impor-tant is multiplying opportunities for expressing differences. Here it is important to notice that Young differentiates rhetoric from deliberation. Rhetoric as an expression of immediate interests is more democratic and inclusive than deliberation. It figures centrally in Young's conception of communicative democracy because rhetoric concerns itself with the situatedness and desires of an audience (71). Driven by more than a concern for deliberation, rhetoric provides opportunities for expressing both the pull of ideas on our emotions and the particular emotional commitments we have to each other. Young concludes that rhetoric—along with storytelling and greeting—provides for particularity and difference, the "expression and extension of shared understandings, where they exist, and the offering and acknowledgment of unshared meanings" (74).

The claims of Mansbridge, Walzer, and Young suggest the kinds of talk among citizens that sustain a democracy are less singularly deliberative and decidedly more amorphous, including seemingly everything and anything. Inclusion in everyday talk, in protest, in greeting, and in storytelling does not necessarily ease the experience of feeling vulnerable to the demands deliberation places on generosity and resources, nor does inclusion necessarily augment the sense of agency or sovereignty that comes from struggling to participate in deliberation. Taking seriously these amendments to and refinements of deliberation leads us to realize that the rhetoric that sustains a democracy is not primarily, or even most importantly, the talk of sovereign citizens taking collective responsibility for making decisions affecting their lives together. Rhetoric requires more than deliberation and seems as a result to be something other than the exercise of collective authority over the common good. Rhetoric is instead something open-ended, an activity which is expressive and performative, an activity through which people fashion commitments without making decisions, an activity through which they express their differences without feeling obligated to affirm their commonalities, an activity through which they come to experience themselves—for better and for worse—as more, not less, open to each other.

Salazar's South African sovereign citizen confronts many of the same constraints and concerns regarding democratic rhetoric. The examples he uses in *An African Athens*, drawn from government, business, and the media—with the exception of the writing of the Constitution of South Africa—are less examples of deliberation and more instances of the kinds of democratically vital nondeliberative discourses highlighted by Mansbridge, Walzer, and Young. His argument seems in fact to be that it is rhetorics of ceremony and memorialization and reconciliation, not the discourses of deliberation, that define the current South African democracy. At the same time Salazar's attention to the one clear example of deliberation, the writing of the constitution, begins by explicitly questioning the applicability of Gutmann and Thompson's conception of democratic deliberation to South Africa (An African Athens, 54) and ends by stating that rhetorics of reconciliation and valuation matter more than deliberation to the South African quest for a common good. Neither Salazar's examples nor his handling of them disproves the lack of or need for meaningful opportunities for South African citizens to deliberate. Nonetheless the fact that he makes his argument through examples of largely non-deliberative discourses would seem to confirm the point made by Mansbridge, Walzer, and Young that other kinds of non-deliberative discourses are vital to a healthy democracy and that the nature of participation in any healthy democracy can not be limited to deliberations about the common good.

This is not to say Salazar is inconsistent or that he should revise his description of rhetoric in South African democracy as both inclusive and deliberative. Neither is it to say that the role of rhetoric in achieving a common good is so amorphous that any account we can give of it—however weak it may be—is the best we can do. Instead it is to say the rhetorical dimensions of citizen sovereignty are not so easily discerned because the nature of meaningful participation in a democracy does not necessarily follow from ideas about inclusion in such activities as public deliberations. The kinds of rhetorical sovereignty a citizen may enjoy are not necessarily yoked in any one given way to specific opportunities for inclusion or modes of deliberation. We need to do more to understand sovereignty, inclusivity, and deliberation in general and in South African democracy in particular in order to give a fuller account of the role of rhetoric in the transition from apartheid.

Common sense tells us that in post-apartheid South Africa thinking about inclusion makes sense as a starting point for understanding the rhetorical agency of the sovereign citizen. Focus on inclusion makes sense in post-apartheid South Africa because it expresses immediate awareness of the recent past of apartheid as undemocratic, as an exclusion that silenced countless voices—an institutionalized disregard for inclusion and an intolerance of deliberative difference. But the desire to emphasize inclusion in order to avoid the exclusions of apartheid provides only a negative outline of the sovereignty of the democratic citizen, as in the preamble of the Constitution of South Africa which states the goals of South African democracy to "Heal the divisions of the past and establish a society based on democratic values, social justice, and fundamental human rights," to "Lay the foundations for a democratic and open society in which government is based on the will of the people and every citizen is equally protected under the law," to "Improve the quality of life of all citizens and free the potential of each person," and to "Build a united and democratic South Africa able to take its rightful place as a sovereign state in the family of nations." This sensitivity to overcoming a past of exclusion—as important as it is—by itself provides little in the way of looking forward toward articulating all the conditions needed for realizing a future of inclusiveness. If we heed Young's argument that banning exclusions—such as those that defined apartheid—does not in and of itself do enough to enable inclusion, then we see that we are obligated to identify and develop positive terms for citizen sovereignty if we are to assess as well as promote inclusion in democratic rhetoric in South Africa—or anywhere for that matter.

As I have presented him here Salazar earnestly wants appeals to rhetoric to do just this kind of work and provide a full positive definition of the terms of inclusion for sovereign citizens that is appropriate to and meaningful beyond South Africa. Those appeals become less helpful the longer we consider them because the opportunities for rhetorical participation vital to a healthy democracy cannot be so easily tamed and do in fact become so expansive that they become detached from the immediate circumstances of citizens discretely and purposefully exercising their sovereignty, such as in democratic deliberations over land reparation. It is in large part the lack of direct influence that uses of words have on material circumstances that leads so many to be critical of the TRC and South African democracy. I think letting the persistence of inequality drive skepticism of the contributions that words have made to the democratic transition misconstrues the role rhetoric has played and can play in nurturing a common ground shared by all. The nature of rhetoric's role in a democracy is nothing we can agree on in order to settle once and for all the terms for inclusion and the meaning of sovereign participation. For this reason I want to step back from the ambition to fully define the conditions for inclusion in order to approach from a different angle the issue of rhetoric's role in shaping South African democracy.

Just as the South African Constitution grounds its human rights claims in contrast to an apartheid past, an honest evaluation of the potential in rhetoric for giving a positive description of what a democratic citizen should in fact do requires of us that we pay attention to what the description is intended to overcome. Viewed in this way we see that a description of the sovereign citizen as someone having rights and responsibilities where there were once none, as in the case of South African citizenship after apartheid—a negation of the negation of inclusion—carries forward with it a continued awareness of the conditions of vulnerability upon which that sovereignty is asserted. Sensitivity to the vulnerabilities of exclusion may not by itself provide a compelling or complete definition of democracy, but neither is fully articulating the terms for inclusion a final guarantee of democratically meaningful citizenship. Even if we could through inclusion eliminate the vulnerabilities associated with exclusion we would not therefore eliminate any and all vulnerabilities. Inclusion in democratic deliberations is not necessarily a guarantee of sovereign control over self and circumstances. Full participation in democratic deliberations necessarily makes citizens vulnerable to the vicissitudes of interacting with others. Deliberation can be structured in ways that are more or less alien to citizens, with the result that decisions arrived at deliberatively will make more or less sense and seem more or less fair, leaving citizens feeling more or less vulnerable to the will of others. The example of land reparations is a good case in point. Even under the best deliberative conditions imaginable, there will be citizens who will not obtain reparations, whose continued material insecurity will result from their participation in deciding what is in the best interest of all. In reality, as tempting as it is to want to structure inclusion in deliberations as a remedy to all the kinds of exclusions that limit sovereign citizenship, vulnerabilities persist that talk among citizens can not resolve.

Even though people may at times find themselves at odds with their fellow citizens, living with the vulnerabilities attending inclusion in a democracy is not necessarily a bad thing. Patchen Markell expresses the point well, echoing Salazar's characterization of democratic deliberation by highlighting the demand democracy makes on everyone to shoulder a "share of the burden and risk involved in the uncertain, open-ended, sometimes maddeningly and sometimes joyously surprising activity of living and interacting with other people" (7). Burden and risk. Uncertainty and open-endedness. Even in a democracy everyone is bound to abide by decisions they might not agree with, face up to situations and decisions they might not fully comprehend, decisions that might cause them distress or hardship or even relief and joy, whether or not they were able to actively and effectively deliberate in making those decisions. What is at issue then in advocating for the roles of deliberation and persuasion in a democracy is not only the matter of assuring the highest level of citizen sovereignty by promoting the greatest degree of inclusion. Also at issue is the matter of discerning how through uses of rhetoric—through expressing the desire for inclusion and exercising communicative sovereignty—democratic citizens come to share the burden and risk of belonging. The issue is one of them finding a way to decide among themselves how they will manage the inescapability of their vulnerabilities to each other. Another more accurate way to put it would be to say that cultivating citizen sensitivity to vulnerabilities is more important to achieving democratic participation than realizing ambitions for sovereign inclusion.

In what follows I argue for understanding rhetoric as a resource useful in the managing of experiences of vulnerability in South Africa. I use the term "rhetoric" in a broad sense to connote the deliberative, expressive, and persuasive activities of representing and making sense—for ourselves and with each other—of our ambitions, circumstances, concerns, and disappointments, as well as our fears and hopes and values. I focus on vulnerability because the quest to achieve sovereignty—understood as a freedom from constraints on willful action—does not eradicate vulnerability as much as it transforms it. None of us is ever so sovereign that we become invulnerable.

Questions of vulnerability and sovereignty dominate the history of South Africa. As part of an effort to assert national sovereignty, the racial classifications grounding apartheid policies were expressions of Afrikaner perceptions of their own vulnerability. Racial classifications were managed by the apartheid government as a means to provide guarantees from insecurities of status and to secure self-determination for Afrikaners, primarily through control of the geographic isolation of the majority African population into distinct racial groups. To miss that the policies of apartheid were coercive compensation for the anxiety of Afrikaners over the paucity of their claims to authority, influence, and resources is to miss how rhetoric and violence work together to shape South African society. More than this, it is to miss how rhetoric functioned in the resistance to and eventual collapse of the apartheid government. If apartheid was a displacement and concentration of vulnerability onto the non-white population of South Africa, then the struggle against apartheid was more than simply a struggle for African self-determination. The struggle against apartheid—as a struggle for self-determination—was a struggle to redefine the terms of that self-determination, a struggle against a rhetoric of securing claims for sovereignty by displacing vulnerability onto others.

Despite Afrikaner fears of their own vulnerability after the transition to democracy, fears that they would as a minority racial group be made more vulnerable in a democracy, the struggle for a democratic South Africa was a struggle to find more inclusive terms for distributing and organizing authority and influence as well as susceptibility to authority and influence in a post-apartheid public life shared by everyone. To understand the role of rhetoric in apartheid, in the liberation struggle, and in the birth as well as growth of a democratic South Africa is to recognize more generally the challenges of distributing and organizing sovereignty and vulnerability. Central to such an understanding is an enlarged sense of what constitutes both aspirations for sovereignty and conditions of vulnerability. According to this enlarged sense sovereignty and vulnerability condition each other in such a way that aspirations for sovereignty are checked and conditions of vulnerability are made more apparent within the arena of words. This is not to suggest a disregard for the consequences of persistent material inequality on the quality of South African democracy. But neither is it to disregard—as many materialists do—the contributions of language to the health of South African democracy. To understand the intertwining of the ambition for participatory sovereignty with the persistence of material vulnerability is instead to acknowledge the consequences our deployment of the resources of persuasion and coercion in public life have for our experiences and understandings of ourselves with others. Unless we attend in this way to the role of rhetoric we misconstrue our ambitions for sovereignty over ourselves, our acceptance of and resignation to our vulnerability to the actions and motivations of others (especially as these actions and motivations are given authority and accumulate power through traditions and institutions), as well as our senses of and hope for progress in managing the conditions for sovereignty and of vulnerability. By attending to the rhetorics of struggle against apartheid and of the emergence of democracy in South Africa, this book develops an account of the importance of understanding rhetoric in public life as a managing of a vulnerability that includes, but is not limited to, susceptibility to the sufferings of hardship as well as to the suffering of appeals from others. The next chapter provides a more complete outline of this conception of vulnerability in order to ground the remaining chapters and their discussions of specific instances in the struggle to shape shared rhetorical sovereignty in democratic South Africa.

Chapter 2

RHETORIC AS VULNERABILITY

To get a better sense of both the concern for vulnerability that motivates an ambition for rhetorical sovereignty and the vulnerabilities that nonetheless attend inclusion it is useful to return to Salazar's appeal to theories of rhetoric and the experience of democratic participation in South Africa. What makes this a productive point of departure is that Salazar makes a dual move. He draws on resources in rhetoric to reflect on democracy in South Africa at the same time that he expands on rhetoric's resources through their application in South Africa. Salazar is well aware of the dual move and in his introduction to a special issue of the journal *Quest* dedicated to "rhetorical approaches to democratic deliberation" he is positive about the possibilities of both "acclimatizing" rhetoric to South Africa and contributing to scholarship on South African democracy.

The *Quest* issue dedicated to rhetoric that begins with Salazar's hope for rhetoric in South Africa ends interestingly with Wim van Binsbergen's urgings that the theory of rhetoric is geographically, historically, and intellectually so distinct from South African experience that appeals to rhetoric function as nothing more than further colonizations of African experiences of democracy and deliberation. Responding to the volume as a whole, Binsbergen concludes, "the suggestion of another hegemonic assault, this time in the name of Aristotle and rhetoric, must be avoided at all costs" (264). For Binsbergen bringing rhetorical theory to South African democratic experience fails because it undervalues indigenous resources he considers definitive of sovereignty in South Africa. His view that experience must speak to and through theory leads him to dismiss rhetoric as an imposition of meaning beside the point in South Africa,

"The point is, therefore, *not* that the contributors to this volume . . . should be faulted for advocating a rhetoric-based perspective; the point is that they have just left it to others to sort out how such a perspective could be combined with other valuable perspectives such as the anti-hegemonic and comparative Africanist one" (265). In the end Binsbergen is not ready to accept the need for rhetoric to define sovereignty in South Africa until more attention is given to what he characterizes as Africanist perspectives.

Binsbergen has good reason to be sensitive to a colonization of sovereign experience through theory, particularly rhetorical theory. As V. Y. Mudimbe has shown, the imposition of meaning onto Africa has propelled and been propelled by European exploitation of the continent. To move beyond distorted characterizations of Africa as the barbaric other of first ancient Greece and then modern Europe, Mudimbe like Binsbergen argues for the experience of Africa to be given expression in African, not European, terms.

But the opposition of indigenous to colonial is as fraught as that between the sovereign and the vulnerable that it is mobilized to serve. As Mahmood Mamdani argues, framing the choice between European and Africanist perspectives hinders rather than helps resolve issues of democratic sovereignty on the African continent because it instantiates a historically unrealistic opposition between the vulnerability of exclusion from political power and the sovereignty of inclusion in colonial power. Mamdani explains that European colonization did not simply assert the African as an excluded Other. The colonization of Africa was instead realized through creation of tribal African authorities who participated in and helped perpetuate colonial European authority and legitimacy. He puts it most clearly when he writes, "the subject population was incorporated into—and not excluded from—the arena of colonial power" (15). Because Mamdani understands the current crisis of democratization on the African continent as more than a matter of past exclusion or even marginalization as such, he rejects as viable solutions both greater opportunities for political inclusion and what he considers nostalgia for traditional authorities that are in reality indigenous only to colonial Africa. Instead the problem and so the solution turn on diagnosing and dismantling a "mode of rule organized on the basis of fused power, administrative justice, and extra-economic coercion, all legitimized as the customary" (296). For Mamdani the solution involves rearticulating the sovereignty of citizenship and vulnerabilities of subjectivity through a critical reformulation of the African civil sphere.

Aletta Norval observes as well that apartheid "did not operate either through logics of exclusion, nor simply through differential forms of inclusion, but through the simultaneous retention of both these logics" (10). Norval describes the democratic resolution of apartheid as a reformulation of the logics of exclusion and inclusion, a reformulation that "calls forth a responsibility for keeping open the space of contestation of identification" (304), such that the "possibility of contestation" and a "democratic ethos" become normative (305). What Mamdani and Norval expose is the reality that oppositional logics of inclusive and exclusive, foreign and indigenous, misconstrue the conditions of apartheid and so prevent us from recognizing that achieving democracy requires more than working toward achieving greater participation in defining a common good: achieving democracy involves a reformulation of the sovereignty that comes with inclusion and an acceptance of the vulnerabilities that attend responsibility for contesting the limits of shared conditions and identities.

The question I am most concerned with here is whether rhetorical activity and understanding provide a tool useful for just such a reformulation. There is no inherent reason rhetoric cannot function productively with concerns over sovereignty and vulnerability in the African context. One way to understand Salazar's move to acclimatize rhetoric to Africa is to recognize it as an attempt to make good on Mamdani's insight by evolving rhetorical theory into a viable resource for expressing South African experiences of citizenship and democracy. As useful as they are, Salazar's efforts to acclimatize rhetoric to Africa do not go quite far enough in this direction because his ambition for sovereignty through inclusion in a post-apartheid democracy does not adequately account for those vulnerabilities that persist and that derive from somewhere other than past exclusions.

Erik Doxtader's efforts to develop a rhetorical understanding of the work of the TRC are more sensitive to the inescapable contingencies and continuing vulnerabilities attending the transition from apartheid to democracy in South Africa. It is important to note up front that the institutionalization of reconciliation in the offices of the TRC is deeply complex and involves many people in many different roles. Doxtader nowhere claims that his appeals to rhetoric to theorize the work of reconciliation exhaust the meaning and significance of the experience of all South Africans. Quite the opposite. In his essay on the history of the concept of reconciliation in South Africa—"Making Rhetorical History in a Time of Transition"—Doxtader carefully documents the multiple formulations of reconciliation, all the while noting that his genealogy does not exhaust the meanings and uses of the term. As he characterizes his argument, "reconciliation took shape as its proponents used argumentation to defend the proposition that citizens could overcome violence and realize concrete political change if they were willing to practice a kind of communication. As reconciliation was held to be a trope of resistance, compromise, and deliberation, the form and substance of this communication about communication varied" (225–26). What rhetorical theory brings to Doxtader's understanding of the South African experience of reconciliation is an account of the power of words to trump violence. As he most clearly puts it, his essay "plots how advocates of reconciliation defined the force of time, the ways in which reconciliation created temporal frames in order to forge the potential for communication from within threats of violence" (227).

As much as we may be willing to accept that the variety of discourses of reconciliation contributed to containing violence and motivating democracy, Doxtader is hard pressed to draw out of his appeal to rhetoric an account of how or why those discourses functioned as they did. There is as he notes in the conclusion of his essay, quoting a young South African artist, something magical about the transition from apartheid to democracy (252). The reference to magic is more than an expression of wonder, it is also a recognition on Doxtader's part that the emergence of democracy in South Africa cannot be reductively explained through appeal to the sovereign exercise of rhetoric. The fact of citizen participation and deliberation does not alone account for the miracle of democracy in South Africa. Neither can the magic of the transition be explained through appeal to immediate experience. This need not discourage analysis. The remainder of wonder is no reason to forego our efforts at explanation. So I think Doxtader is fair in being adamant that, "We cannot do with the banal notion that reconciliation appeared out of thin air, a concept without deep roots or a practice that has not been thoughtfully contested on the South African landscape. The negotiated revolution made time for speech. The terms of this rhetorical transition must play some role in our assessments as to what this speech has made" (254). The question of what speech has made asks at least two things: what account can we give of language's capacity for effecting change, and at the same time, what account can we give of ourselves as manipulators of language's capacity for effecting change?

While these two versions of the question are related, they are also distinct. The question of language's capacity for effecting change is a question of our acceptance of or susceptibility to language as an agent of change. It is a question of whether and how words touch us. The question of our capacity for using language to effect change is a question of our accepting responsibility for uses to which we put words. It is a question of whether and how we make use of words to touch others, or, recalling Salazar's term, whether and how we act as sovereign citizens who participate productively in the public expression of a common good. The possibility in language for the unintended consequences of our uses of words complicates the question of rhetorical sovereignty with the acknowledgement that our words can have an impact we could not have fore-seen and might not want to take responsibility for. It is this feature of language that cautions Doxtader's claim. On the one hand he seems to want to say along with Salazar that talk about reconciliation functioned as a resource for use by people participating in the collective expressing of a common good. On the other hand he seems to be aware we do not have sovereignty over the effects of our words, that we are vulnerable to our words and to the sovereignty our words do at times have over us. Awareness of our simultaneous sovereignty over and vulnerability to words may seem to limit the sense it makes to appeal to rheto-ric to provide a resource for citizens participating in fashioning the common good, but awareness of the duplicity of language actually provides more subtle insight into the experiences of deeds done in words. The perspective admitting of our vulnerability to expression in the face of our ambition for sovereignty over meaning refuses along with Mamdani and Norval the binary logic of inclusion and exclusion and in so doing makes rhetorical theory a more subtle approach to comprehending the transition from apartheid to democracy, an approach that avoids defining inclusion as nothing more than establishing the baseline conditions for extending to all citizens equal opportunities for civic participation.

In his contribution to the *Quest* issue on rhetoric in South Africa—"Works of Faith, Faith of Works"—Doxtader elaborates his argument about the rheto-ric of reconciliation by narrowing his attention to the TRC's definition of rec-onciliation as forgiveness. Doing so he gets right at the issues of our sovereignty over and vulnerability to the words we use. He affirms Archbishop Desmond Tutu's insistence that reconciliation as forgiveness cannot be had cheaply and so must therefore "be explained such that it does not appear as a sacrifice that exacerbates the reality of apartheid injustice" (51). The sovereign capacity to forgive is for Doxtader a rhetorical act. Forgiveness is "a mode of discovery and invention, a speech-act in which victims of violence are able to re-present their historical identities in a manner that cultivates both the potential (dunamis) and the ethos of collective interaction" (51). Understood in these terms, for-giveness is a generative act willfully engaged in. Forgiveness gives to apartheid's victims a power to participate in cultivating collective interaction—it enacts and affirms a sense of sovereignty—but Doxtader is well aware that extend-ing forgiveness also requires of those same victims a hard acceptance of their vulnerability. Referencing remarks made by TRC Human Rights Commissioner Pumla Gobodo-Madikizela, Doxtader acknowledges the pain that attends tes-timony detailing personal experiences of human rights abuses, "This show of vulnerability—re-living past trauma on a public stage but with uncertain audience—led [Gobodo-Madikizela] to note that the hearings were at times brutal and sometimes seemed bizarre and heartless" (52).

The brutality and heartlessness in the testimonies of victimization trouble the hope that participation in the TRC was at its best a democratic exercise in citizen sovereignty. Victims need not forgive those who committed human rights abuses against them. Not all who appeared to testify before the TRC were willing or even able to do so. As Martha Minow puts it, "Forgiveness is a power held by the victimized, not a right to be claimed. The ability to dispense, but also to withhold, forgiveness is an ennobling capacity and part of the dignity to be reclaimed by those who survive the wrongdoing. . . . To expect survivors to forgive is to heap yet another burden on them" (17). Recognizing the need to respect the rights of victims to not participate is important to understanding the nature of their potential sovereignty and their perpetual vulnerability. No one need forgive. But as Gobodo-Madikizela points out, victims who hang on to feelings of resentment, who cannot forgive, may not know what else to do. The emotions of anger and desire for vengeance can become "a symbol of the perpetrator's powerful grip over the victim, they are a burden that hangs over the victim and at once creates a dependency on the hateful emotions and denies the victim a chance to come to terms with what happened" (96). For Gobodo-Madikizela the act of forgiving is an opportunity for openness to others, a kind of reversal of the vulnerability the victim experienced at the hands of the victimizer. It can enact what she terms a "paradox of remorse" in which a victim empathizes with the pain of regret felt by the perpetrator (100). Forgiveness can in this way also lead to dialogue that enacts the humanizing of the perpetrator, a process that is both "punishment and rehabilitation" (120). In addition to humbling and humanizing the perpetrator, dialogue allows the victim of human rights abuse to feel more human as well, providing a "process of reclaiming self-efficacy," in which "reciprocating with empathy and forgiveness in the face of the perpetrator's remorse restores to many victims the sense that they are once again capable of effecting a profound difference in the moral community" (128). Even though forgiveness promises a contribution to the moral order and we may hope for the best in people to be brought out through forgiveness, we must always remember that we cannot expect it. The open-endedness of forgiveness provides no guarantees. Citing the Holocaust historian Saul Friedlander, Minow cautions against "giving in to the temptations of closure, because that would avoid what remains inevitably indeterminate, elusive, and inexplicable about collective horrors" (24).

Without in any way discounting the experiences of those who publicly testified to their victimization, it is worth adding here that the experience of hearing seemingly endless testimony of human rights abuses took its toll on those who listened. Gobodo-Madikizela explains that many of those who served on the TRC continue to struggle with their own emotional closure because they had to deny their own emotions in order to contain the pain of victims appearing before them (94). As Krog explains, reporters following the TRC suffer from the strain as well, becoming ill, feeling alienated from families and friends. All this is to say the act of forgiving and the witnessing of someone forgiving are not experienced by all as entirely constructive. In the experience of those who participated in the TRC these were no doubt experienced at times as far more painful than productive. Yet people did risk the pain of participating in the TRC because doing so held out the promise of a sense of connectedness that would restore in South Africans hope for their lives together. The pain and the joy of, as Krog put it, participating in "the birth of this country's language itself" (42), or in Gobodo-Madikizela's words, learning "a vocabulary of compromise and tolerance," was a vital part of the project of democratization, in which citizens settle "differences through the politics of contestation and compromise among equals," a process that "seeks to create new relationships and repair old ones" (126).

Doxtader synthesizes the sovereignty of forgiving with the vulnerability of forgiving through descriptive appeal to the TRC's theological formulations of reconciliation as forgiveness: "as we recognize our dependence on God and neighbour, forgiveness appears as a productive vulnerability. The abandonment of sovereign identity allows humans to redress oppression through a (paradoxical) relation of difference" ("Works of Faith," 54). Providing more secular theoretical terms to account for the necessity of productive vulnerability, Doxtader appeals to Hannah Arendt's notion of forgiveness, extracting from it acknowledgment that "The power of creativity, the initiative of beginning, comes at the cost of self-sufficiency. This lack is the motive and necessity of forgiveness" (56). Here vulnerability and sovereignty motivate each other. To stop the authority of words over our lives requires taking on the burden of rhetorically fashioning a new meaning others may not acknowledge or accept. To accept the possibility of experiencing words differently requires risking what are surely unknown consequences. As sovereign rhetorical agents vulnerable to the rhetoric of others, we are, in Doxtader's words, "doers and sufferers both simultaneously" (56).

For Arendt the human capacity to forgive is an essential feature of the sovereignty of humans acting in the unpredictable presence of others. Forgiving provides the ability to intervene in preventing the unforeseen consequences of our actions echoing endlessly into the future (237). With the ability to constrain the consequences of our actions, we are able to initiate different actions.

Forgiving concludes cycles of hatred and vengeance by enacting something new and unexpected. Forgiving is, according to Arendt, "the only reaction which does not merely re-act but acts anew and unexpectedly, unconditioned by the act which provoked it and therefore freeing from its consequences both the one who forgives and the one who is forgiven" (241). To forgive is to make a choice, to act as a sovereign agent, to begin again. Forgiveness is not conditioned by past action; it is not a future to be expected from a past that has been given us. As a result the act of forgiving initiates a new beginning; it signals a willingness to be open to others and their actions. Among those who seek forgiveness it is a desire to reclaim the possibility of interacting with others. It is an effort to grope toward a common good. But forgiving is more than an assertion, it is also an openness, an accepting and so a managing of vulnerability.

Putting it in terms of rhetoric, Doxtader writes, "Cast as a performative act of recognition . . . the logic of forgiveness shows an important rhetorical charac- ter, a tropological movement between the discovery of identity and the appear- ance of opposition that funds the invention of human identification" ("Works of Faith," 57). Through identification and opposition people strive to achieve a common good, and in that striving forgiveness becomes "an expression of faith in which the power of creativity is situated in a heartfelt commitment to mutuality that less fiats over difference than draws from it to reveal the necessity of human interaction" (58). Commitments to mutuality and interaction real- ized through acts of forgiveness are encouraged in the TRC specifically through appeal to the notion of *ubuntu*: the African notion that we become human through our relationships with others. The privileging of interconnectedness and the appeal to *ubuntu* in many important South African documents such as the South African Constitution and the final report of the TRC replace the rigid vulnerability of apartheid racial identity with the contingent vulnerability of human interaction.

Appeal to *ubuntu* is a way of making claims for rights and resources explic- itly contingent on relationships with others whose own claims for rights and resources do overlap and may create conflict. It is a way of leaving people to decide among themselves which of their claims are more justified by asking them to all share equally in making decisions about who should be made vul- nerable, and when, to the vicissitudes of civic life. In post-apartheid South Africa vulnerability has been made into an explicit topic people must take account of and manage among themselves as they go through their lives together. They must discuss among themselves and make decisions about who gets what resources, when, and why. The conversations required to manage the sharing of vulnerability are typically not easy. Faith in *ubuntu* and commitment to inter-connectedness does not always provide guidance for these conversations and can even become strained by them. Nonetheless the opportunity to have such conversations is always preferable to having vulnerability assigned beforehand and without input.

Before the TRC provided a national forum for what Michael Battle describes as Desmond Tutu's *ubuntu* theology, leaders of the apartheid government and the resistance struggle who motivated the transition from apartheid to democracy recognized the necessity of interacting with each other for the sake of the future of the country. Trusting in the benefits of words, all sides in the negotiated settlement risked mutual trust in others they had come to learn they could not trust. As the negotiations for peaceful transition proceeded, however haltingly, the violent struggle between the apartheid government and its opponents worsened. At the same time neither side wanted a protracted civil war that would destroy the country. A resolution through rhetoric held out the only hope for avoiding all-out civil war and providing security from violence while ensuring the stability of the country. Each side had its own reasons for embracing rhetoric instead of clinging to violence. Afrikaners hoped to secure for themselves not only protection from reprisals but also protection of their assets. Africans pinned their hopes for a rhetorical resolution to the transition to Afrikaner cooperation in administering a liberal democratic state. Each side pinned its hopes to rhetoric as a resource which would provide control over the terms of the transition and so secure protection from perceived vulnerabilities to the inevitable demise of apartheid.

Embracing rhetoric and mobilizing its resources so as to avoid bloodshed or imprisonment or displacement meant accepting the contingency of openness to others. The attempt to exchange vulnerability to violence for vulnerability to the claims and interests and needs and values of others is not any kind of escape from vulnerability. Nor does it even necessarily remove vulnerability from a physically terrifying place to a politically tolerable one. As a good number of critics of the negotiated settlement and transition to democracy have observed, gross inequalities in the distribution of wealth and resources that defined apartheid have persisted almost unabated through the transition to democracy. David Howarth put the point best by distinguishing the transition to democracy in South Africa from what has yet to be attempted, a more fundamental and more ambitious democratic transformation, a "longer-term process of restructuring the underlying social relations" (203). Gobodo-Madikizela put it this way, "True social transformation—and healing of victims—will come about only if the issues of economic justice and the myriad problems that post-apartheid South Africa faces are addressed" (126).

The possibility that the democratic transition is both a testament to the potential power of rhetoric and an example of the intractability of economic inequality suggests less the impotence of words and more the thick intertwining of the rhetorical authority people have over their lives and over the conditions of their existence with the persistence of vulnerability to those conditions and to the people with whom they share their lives. Celebrating rhetoric's role in securing the transition to democracy is more than a kind of self-congratulatory disregard for the poverty that persists. South Africans do like anyone else need to be able to tell themselves that their choice of words over violence is a good trade on their vulnerability to each other. There can be no doubt that in many ways it is. At the same time, in our efforts to promote democratization through an understanding of rhetoric we should not let opportunities for participation lead us to ignore what rhetoric has not done and perhaps cannot do to transform the material conditions of people's lives. A more nuanced understanding of the intertwining of rhetorical agency and material existence is provided by acknowledging rhetoric's functioning as a managing of vulnerability, as a commitment to the sharing of words that does not entirely remove us from threats of daily insecurity and violence even as it does bring with it the additional vulnerabilities associated with opening our individual fates to our interactions with others.

In the following chapters I seek to understand the intertwining of rhetorical efficacy with vulnerabilities to material existence by beginning with attention to a rhetorical artifact, a textual trace of an aspiration for sovereignty or expression of vulnerability. In each case, I explore the resonance of a single rhetorical artifact through South African life. Doing so, I hope to encourage a sensitivity to the ambitions and ambivalences of struggling for the sovereignty of expression without surrendering vulnerability to all that expression entails. This rationale dictates as well the artifacts to be discussed. In the next chapter I draw on the silencing of Robert Sobukwe to understand the struggle against apartheid as a struggle against a rhetoric securing sovereignty through the displacement of vulnerability. I begin with Sobukwe because of his view that black South Africans were responsible for their own liberation. Sobukwe was the first president of the Pan Africanist Congress, a splinter organization of the African National Congress. He was also responsible for organizing the boycott of pass laws that culminated in the Sharpeville massacre on March 21, 1960. My claim is that Sobukwe's appeal to black South Africans was not an appeal to simply wrest authority from white South Africans. Rather, the struggle against apartheid was more importantly a struggle for a rhetoric of accepting vulnerability as the condition all must share for democratic sovereignty.

I build on my claim regarding Sobukwe by attending to the rhetoric of Robben Island, a place made infamous during apartheid as the place where the government held those who resisted its policies. As such Robben Island served as a point of geographic reference for the displacement of vulnerability. Since the end of apartheid Robben Island has come to serve as a point for geographically rearticulating the terms of sovereignty out of conditions of vulnerability. South Africans must always be susceptible to Robben Island rhetoric for it to persuade them of their democratic sovereignty. I turn from discussing Robben Island to explore the controversy surrounding the proposed Freedom Monument—a cast of Mandela's open hand reaching skyward through prison bars—and then consider the nature of compromise by describing the antipathies and sympathies in democratic South Africa that gained expression through debate about the memorialization of the liberation struggle. To extend the discussion of antipathies and sympathies I take up issues regarding compromise and forgiveness in the discourse surrounding the Truth and Reconciliation Commission (TRC). Chairman of the TRC, Archbishop Desmond Tutu, was uncompromising in his opposition to apartheid and in his support of reconciliation through forgiveness. The challenge of what Tutu characterized as his "even-handedness" is captured in Pumla Gobodo-Madikizela's sympathetic gesture of touching Eugene de Kock, the former leader of apartheid secret police. In her gesture of regard for the vulnerability of apartheid's most notorious assassin, Gobodo-Madikizela gives expression to the personal dimensions of rhetorical sovereignty and vulnerability. Her encounter with de Kock exemplifies Tutu's conflation of even-handedness with the African notion of *ubuntu*—that we only become human through the humanity of others. I conclude my argument from artifacts with two filmic representations of reconciliation: *District 9* and the film version of Athol Fugard's novel, *Tsotsi*. In both films the protagonists discover their humanity through their encounters with others. In *Tsotsi*, the main character, David, finds his humanity through his vulnerability first to an infant, then to a young widow living in his township, and finally to the infant's father. The ambivalence of David's awakening to his humanity—and so to his sovereignty—is played out in narrative tension with his becoming vulnerable to collective demands for justice. In *District 9,* the main character, Wikus van der Merwe, finds his humanity only upon his metamorphosis into an extraterrestrial. He finds his humanity in his alienation from his Afrikaner heritage. Taken together, the narratives of personal discovery of an African and an Afrikaner give expression to the shared vulnerabilities required for the success of reconciliatory rhetoric.

As parts of a whole, the artifacts discussed provide a description of the larger role of rhetoric—its prospects as well as its perils—in the building and sustaining of democracy in South Africa. This range of expressions of individual passion and collective need makes clear beyond the borders of the experience of South Africans just how fragile our common good really is.

Chapter 3

THE DANGEROUS RHETORIC
OF ROBERT SOBUKWE

On April 24, 1963, South African Minister of Justice Johannes Balthazar Vorster introduced legislation to the parliament of the Republic of South Africa. Regarding Clause 4 of the General Amendment Bill, he told the assembly:

> Honorable members are as aware as I am that Sobukwe will have served his sentence on 3 May. If Honorable members have read their newspapers they will know as well as I do that he was firstly the leader of the P.A.C. and I can tell Honorable members there has been no change of heart in him during the time he has not been in our midst. I want to put it to Honorable members candidly, so they can place themselves in my position. If the Government—and the Government has to consider this matter—comes to the conclusion, having regard to the circumstances as they have developed, and the facts as exposed in the Snyman Commission Report, that it would be failing in its duty to the peaceful citizenry if it were to set this man free. This clause will be used to keep him there longer. Sir, I know it is challengeable. I know the principle is that here is a man who has served his sentence. But having regard to the circumstances, the Government may decide that it may be necessary for the security of the state to do so. For here we are dealing with a person—let me say this—who has a strong, magnetic personality, a person who can organize, a person who feels that he has a vocation to perform this task, well knowing the methods that will be applied, as I have

told the House earlier. That is the principle of the Clause 4. (RSA Assembly Debates April 24, 1963, p. 4652)

Clause 4 quickly became known as the Sobukwe clause because Robert Sobukwe was the only person to whom it was applied—twice—each time keeping Sobukwe imprisoned three years beyond the end of his sentence. Sobukwe was one of the founders and the first president of the Pan Africanist Congress (PAC), a group that broke away from the African National Congress (ANC) in 1959 over a disagreement regarding the Freedom Charter that outlined ambitions for post-apartheid South Africa, specifically the charter's liberalism.

Under Sobukwe the PAC was responsible for organizing a mass demonstration against the pass laws which required Africans to carry work and travel permits they had to present to police on demand. To protest the pass laws, Sobukwe encouraged Africans to assemble without their passes at police stations across the country, inviting mass arrests intended to paralyze the South African justice system. On March 21, 1960, the protestors who had assembled at the police station in Sharpeville were fired upon by police, who killed 67 and wounded 186. In the days and weeks that followed, protests spread throughout the country. The South African government declared a state of emergency, banned the ANC and PAC, and proceeded to arrest Africans by the thousands.

In 1963, near the end of Sobukwe's three-year sentence for violating the pass laws at the Orlando police station, Vorster introduced the clause he would use to keep Sobukwe in isolation on Robben Island a total of six years beyond the end of his sentence. Presenting the clause to Parliament, Vorster admits the principle represented in it is challengeable. He acknowledges it is unjust to keep a person detained beyond the conclusion of a prison sentence and is aware Sobukwe will have served his three-year sentence. But as Vorster explains, there is more at stake than principle: there are circumstances so dire they require government to abandon principles. This is not to suggest that the apartheid government was principled. Rather it is to observe that officials like Vorster were conscious of maintaining an appearance of adhering to principle, an adherence that required of them explanations for when they may have appeared to act otherwise, which was quite often. The exception is not so exceptional and is in fact the precarious foundation of the apartheid government's claim to sovereignty. So Vorster offers a justification for the Sobukwe clause. He makes a point of the fact that Sobukwe is unrepentant—although one person's lack of repentance hardly seems enough reason for Vorster to appeal to the parliament to so blatantly usurp the rule of law. Sobukwe was no doubt not the only person arrested in the struggle against apartheid who remained unrepentant. Fear that Sobukwe would again become active in the struggle against apartheid may have been a factor in the decision to violate the rule of law, but it could not have been the only factor. Something else was at stake. Other circumstances weighed in the decision to abandon any pretense of principle in Sobukwe's detention.

Circumstances in South Africa in early 1963 were indeed dire. The suppression that followed immediately upon the Sharpeville massacre persuaded many in the struggle against apartheid that nonviolent protest would achieve nothing, encouraging leaders of both the ANC and PAC to turn to violent insurgency. It was soon after Sharpeville that Nelson Mandela began organizing the guerilla wing of the ANC, Umkhonto we Sizwe (MK). In the early years of the 1960s Poqo—the militant arm of PAC—and MK bombed civil service facilities such as post offices and power stations in an attempt to disrupt the government. By mid-year 1963 the government arrested high-level ANC leaders including Mandela and charged them with treason. By 1964, with ANC and PAC leaders imprisoned or living in exile, the organized resistance to apartheid was for a time quelled. Taken together with these circumstances, passage of the Sobukwe clause might be understood as part of a larger strategy to eliminate the leadership of the resistance to apartheid. This was no doubt part of Vorster's intent. Still, however substantial the threat posed to the security of the government by the political and insurgent apartheid resistance, that threat seems too wide-ranging to justify passage of a law aimed at curtailing one man's influence. Circumstances in South Africa in March 1963 were too unstable, protest too widespread and too violent to justify passage of a bill narrowly tailored to keep just one man in prison past the end of his sentence. What was it about Sobukwe in particular that aroused so much fear in the apartheid government? In his introduction of Clause 4, Vorster does not even mention the unrest and violence. He doesn't need to. To maintain its control, the South African government had an apparatus in place adequate to arrest, convict, and detain apartheid's opponents. But Vorster does not appeal to the use of these state resources. Sobukwe is unique. Other options are needed. As Vorster clarifies the circumstances that made Sobukwe so dangerous, he asks the parliament to pay special attention to his "strong, magnetic personality."

Strong. Magnetic. A person who can organize. Someone who commands the resources of rhetoric. What is so dangerous about Sobukwe is his power of persuasion, a power he used to undermine the racialist foundations of apartheid. The fear that one person commanding the resources of rhetoric can disrupt the established order is about as old as rhetoric itself. As Plato argued in the *Republic,* a well-ordered state has an interest in controlling not only rhetoric but all other forms of free expression, including poetry. For Plato the state monopoly

on generating meaning is necessary because it curtails the possibility of someone telling people what they want to hear instead of what the order of the state
needs them to hear. The danger rhetoric poses is the possibility that appeals
to people's individual interests will lead them to put those personal interests
before the interests of the state. Rhetoric is so dangerous because a state in
which there is no appeal to any principle beyond immediate self-interest leads
to all citizens losing the protection that government order provides. In such a
state, each citizen becomes vulnerable to the demands of every other. The fear
of a war of each against all has motivated thinking about the security of the state
from Plato to social contract theorists such as Hobbes and Locke. As Hobbes
most memorably put it, life outside the order imposed by a state is "nasty, brutish, and short."

Apartheid, as an attempt to impose racial order in South Africa, was an effort
to organize protection from the vulnerabilities of a life that is nasty, brutish, and
short—but for white South Africans only. In the racial order of apartheid, Africans were not citizens. They lived as outsiders. They were without protection
and remained vulnerable. Africans lived as transient workers the state wanted
segregated into their own semi-autonomous homelands where resources were
few and life was harsh. In South Africa in 1963 the prospect that someone could
use words to inspire millions of Africans to put their individual interests before
the interests of the state and its white citizens implied the further prospect that
the Afrikaners who had come to power in 1948 would lose their hold on the
country. While Vorster put this fear of intrusion and instability into play in his
introduction of Clause 4, it was not rhetoric in general that he feared, it was
Sobukwe's rhetorical attacks on racialist thinking that he feared in particular.
Clause 4 was not a broad censorship law. It was not a law banning dissent. It was
a clause intended to silence Sobukwe alone.

What made Sobukwe's rhetoric so dangerous is alluded to in the summary
of an interview conducted with him by Durban *Sunday Tribune* reporter Aida
Parker. A pundit for apartheid, Parker observed, "Sobukwe has been described
as 'The Black Verwoerd.' This I can understand. . . . As you enter, as you talk to
him, you gain much the same impression of power, of leadership, as you do
when with South Africa's Prime Minister. Sobukwe has much the same quiet
courtesy, much the same innate charm—and certainly much the same clear,
incisive, trained mind. You are left with the overwhelming impression that, if
this man is one day released, he will, for good or ill, leave his mark on South
African history" (Pogrund, *How Can Man Die Better,* 222–23). Calling Sobukwe
the "black Verwoerd," even comparing him to Verwoerd, the architect of apartheid, seems bizarre at best. Even if Sobukwe had persuasive powers similar to

those of Verwoerd, the differences between the two men could not have been greater. Verwoerd was much older, an Afrikaner nationalist whose parents immigrated to South Africa from the Netherlands when he was two. Sobukwe was over twenty years younger, a native of the Cape Province, who enjoyed tennis and who only became politicized after he entered the university. Verwoerd was the architect of apartheid. Sobukwe rose to become a leader in the struggle to end apartheid. Despite these and other differences it is Sobukwe's powers of persuasion that Parker points to in her comparison of him with Verwoerd. It is a power people consistently made note of, even during Sobukwe's days as a student at Fort Hare University and then as member of the ANC Youth League. It is the power Vorster cautions against. Sobukwe is strong and magnetic, a person who can organize—the black Verwoerd.

Sobukwe's rhetoric is dangerous because it is somehow the antithesis of Verwoerd's rhetoric. The apartheid order that has its roots in the persuasiveness of Verwoerd's rhetoric has as its greatest threat the disruptiveness of Sobukwe's. Comparing the two suggests that Afrikaner fear of Sobukwe is a fear that the rhetoric which establishes order can in different hands be turned to spread disorder. Such a fear assigns to rhetoric too much power, making it into a force that can just as easily sway people one way or another. Accepting the prospect that rhetoric can serve equally well both Verwoerd and Sobukwe does little to tell us why one is compelling to and the other feared by the apartheid government. The government's ability to imprison Sobukwe and Vorster's ability to use legislation to keep Sobukwe imprisoned beyond the end of his sentence weigh against fear of Sobukwe's persuasiveness as the destabilizing other of Verwoerd's rhetoric. Here it is tempting to say that the Afrikaner fear of Sobukwe is fear that he will appeal to Africans in much the same way Verwoerd appealed to Afrikaners, and since Africans far outnumber Afrikaners, the threat of his appeal is nothing more than a recognition among Afrikaners of the untenability of their claim to rule and a sense of the vulnerability of their hold on power.

But this way of understanding it gives rhetoric too little credit, and in doing so does not make enough sense of celebrations of Verwoerd as charming, clear, and incisive. Neither does it make sense of the fear of Sobukwe and the characterization of him as magnetic and as, somehow, the black Verwoerd. Sobukwe's rhetoric was dangerous because it did more than appeal to a receptive black South African audience—even though it did that—while doing something other than threatening the order of the apartheid state—even though it also did that. Sobukwe's rhetoric was dangerous because it drew attention to and called into question the means for managing vulnerability established through apartheid order. To understand in these terms the danger of Sobukwe's rhetoric requires understanding the challenge it posed to a racial order that confidently managed the vulnerability of Afrikaners by displacing that vulnerability onto Africans. To understand the danger posed by Sobukwe's rhetoric requires understanding the managing of vulnerability through apartheid rhetoric. To understand the managing of vulnerability in apartheid rhetoric requires first some understanding of Verwoerd's persuasiveness.

A professor of psychology at the University of Stellenbosch and a fervent advocate of Afrikaner nationalism, Verwoerd was appointed minister of native affairs in 1950. In 1958 he became prime minister of South Africa, a position he held until his assassination on September 6, 1966. Like Sobukwe's, his character was often commented upon. Rykie van Reenen observed his "immense charm" and "razor sharp brain power." In the same interview Verwoerd told her, "one does not have the problem of worrying whether one perhaps could be wrong" (Giliomee, 520; originally quoted in *Die Burger*, Byvoegsel, June 14, 1957). In another interview Verwoerd said much the same thing: "I don't believe in a policy of conciliation. I believe in a policy of conviction" (Giliomee, 519; originally quoted in Deon Geldenhuys, *The Diplomacy of Isolation* [Johannesburg: Macmillan, 1984], 224).

Verwoerd's personal characteristics, his certainty and decisiveness, became synonymous with South African policies. Journalist Piet Cillie put it well when he observed, "Dr. Verwoerd's spiritual make-up was overwhelmingly intellectual: ordered thoughts, clear doctrines, fixed future plans. What was justified and correct in principle, had to be capable of implementation. Obstacles in human nature must give way to regulation and systematization. The ideal must be imposed on society" (Giliomee, 520; originally quoted in David Welsh, "The Executive and the African Population," in *Leadership in the Apartheid State*, ed. David Welsh [Cape Town: Oxford University Press, 1994], 159). Verwoerd's thoughts were ordered, his plans fixed. South African society should be engineered. Verwoerd could not concern himself with the possibility that he could be wrong, especially when struggling to impose apartheid order on human nature. As architect of apartheid Verwoerd acted with assurance in his execution of a plan for the complete segregation of South African life. His zeal for apartheid expressed more than a personal bigotry. South Africa had already been a racially divided state. Prior to the National Party's election to power in 1948 colonial black South Africans were largely disenfranchised. From 1948 on, the systematic legislation and enforcement of a policy of total racial separation gave full legal expression to the legitimizing of white dominance.

Verwoerd's rhetoric, his dogmatism and xenophobia, helped to compel acquiescence to the apartheid ordering of South African life. But compelling is not persuading. Being dogmatic is not the same as being dynamic. Already the comparison with a charismatic Sobukwe seems strained. Verwoerd could not suffer the problem of worrying whether his plan was in any way wrong. Neither could he concern himself with the breadth of his appeal. For him the error and so the source of concern was less in his vision of segregation and more in the threat of intermingling. Verwoerd's vision of South Africa was one of a nation belonging to Afrikaners. According to this vision Africans belonged on the designated homelands of their respective tribes. Living in isolation from each other, Africans and Afrikaners could then be free to strive to achieve their independent ways of life. This was not simply the extreme expression of ethnonationalist ambitions. Those ambitions were themselves an expression as well of an anxiety at the heart of apartheid. As the Afrikaner Reverend Z. R. Mahabane put it after the 1948 elections, apartheid expressed dual feelings of persistent fear for Afrikaner survival and the sense of superiority of Afrikaners over other races, feelings of superiority that justified protecting against Afrikaner fear for survival. (Giliomee, 471).

To characterize Sobukwe as the black Verwoerd expresses a fear that Sobukwe's rhetoric threatened Afrikaner feelings of superiority that were to be stabilized through racial separation. Whatever it might mean for Vorster to have characterized Sobukwe as "magnetic," acknowledging that Afrikaners regarded him from a position of fear and superiority suggests that what was appalling about Sobukwe was conditioned by what made Verwoerd appealing: power, leadership, charm, a trained mind. It is less these characteristics themselves, less the fear of the power of rhetoric itself, and more the fear of an outsider, an African, who might possesses those characteristics and command that rhetoric and reveal the anxiety beneath the superiority. Sobukwe's rhetoric became a threat because its challenge spoke past Afrikaner confidence in their superiority directly to Afrikaner fear for their own survival. Parker's characterization of Sobukwe as the "black Verwoerd" speaks to an awareness of and anxiety about vulnerability at the heart of Afrikaner rhetorical authority.

To be Afrikaner was to be acutely aware of oneself as vulnerable. It was to know the pain and pride of such events as the Great Trek of 1836–54, during which thousands of Afrikaners escaping British rule moved inland from the Cape, where they settled at high cost in human life. To be Afrikaner was to be aware as well that in the early years of the twentieth century rural Afrikaners were undereducated and underemployed and formed a noticeable underclass among white South Africans. Poor Afrikaners who migrated to the urban centers of South Africa in the early years of the twentieth century in search of work often found themselves competing for jobs directly with Africans. Afrikaners often lost out because they did not speak English and Africans could be made to work for less. The language barrier was a sensitive issue in British colonial South Africa because the language and culture of Afrikaners, Afrikaans, effectively isolated Afrikaners from their Dutch heritage as well.

Verwoerd had already appealed to the pride and isolation of Afrikaners through his involvement in promoting the cause of the "poor whites" in South Africa, a cause around which enough white voters rallied to elect the National Party (NP) to power in 1948. The problem of white poverty was so acute that the government funded a study of the problem by the Carnegie Commission in 1929. The commission published its reports in 1932, providing evidence of the extent of the problems of white poverty in South Africa. While the Carnegie Commission did recognize that the problems of poverty were not black or white but primarily economic in nature, the government responded with greater attention to the poverty of whites, a vast majority of whom were Afrikaners. The reports proposed enabling greater self-sufficiency for all by improving education, creating more universities, and increasing job opportunities through improvements in local industry. In a speech in 1934 to the Volkskongres, Verwoerd admitted that the poverty of Africans and Afrikaners was intertwined, but he recommended it was in the best interests of the nation's economic well-being that efforts be concentrated on resolving the poverty of whites alone (Giliomee, 351). For Verwoerd the preparation of whites for employment necessarily involved the removal of Africans from competition in the job market by channeling them into cheap physical labor or through the promise of developing opportunities in their own homelands.

The ambition for order in apartheid was an ambition for the sovereignty and security of poor, largely rural Afrikaners. The Afrikaner claim for a sovereign state was not for this reason alone an unequivocally positive assertion. It expressed in positive terms the anxieties and negative feelings of the Afrikaners. The idea of the state satisfied the need to establish a place of belonging. From the tale of the Vortrekkers on, sovereignty was the culmination of a narrative of struggling to belong where Afrikaners had not yet felt they belonged, or at least where they at first had no terms for adequately describing their belonging. The terms of the Afrikaner narrative of identity and belonging out of which they claimed their sovereignty purchased security from the fear for Afrikaner national survival by displacing inferiority onto Africans. Africans were identified with the homelands that were themselves the product of Afrikaner rhetoric. Geographic isolation gave Afrikaners a space of control. In 1951 the South African government defined the territorial boundaries of the eight African nations. To control the migration of Africans from the rural homelands to the urban areas in search of work, the government intensified its enforcement of the pass laws.

The pass laws gave expression to the policy that Africans could only be temporary residents and migrant workers outside the homelands. Pass laws required Africans to carry pass books, work and travel permits which they had to produce for police on demand. The large numbers of Africans who could not produce the appropriate pass documents were extradited to their homelands or to labor on white-owned farms. Instrumentalization of apartheid through enforcement of the pass laws made the coercive force of apartheid real in the lives of Africans. The pass books physically persuaded them of the meaning of Afrikaner sovereignty. Where Afrikaners were convinced of their sovereignty through their conviction to African inferiority, Africans were forced to accept the sovereignty of Afrikaners by having the pass books force them into positions of daily vulnerability.

Pass books acquired immense weight in the daily lives of Africans. With a pass book a person could travel and potentially even work. Without it a person was exposed to the risk of arrest. Africans were forced by daily circumstance to cling to their pass books. They were so terrified of being without the documents that many risked their lives to hold onto them. Some lost their lives in trying to retain them. In response to the story of an African dying in a fire trying to retrieve a pass book, a journalist wrote in *The Golden City Post* in 1959, "But it is not heroism—and certainly nothing like bravado—that can make a man go to his death in an attempt to save a pass book. The motive is simply fear—the realization of what his life will be worth without a reference book. For a reference book has ceased to be a mere form of identification. It is interchangeable with the man himself. At times one is forced to the conclusion that the man himself has less dignity, has less claim to official recognition, than a book" (*The Golden City Post*, February 22, 1959; quoted in Pheko, 30). Attention paid to the pass books by government officials and the police made the documents into inescapable proof of a person's existence and worth. It was not that the book could fully replace the person, for the book could not labor. While the pass books did not do the work done by the people carrying them, the people could not labor without the books. They could not be without them. All they could do was become whoever the books said they were. This was the rhetorical power of the pass books, the authority of the word confirmed in the document that the Afrikaners held over Africans.

As much as Verwoerd participated in creating an Afrikaner identity through a narrative of Afrikaner national culture, that narrative came to incorporate and to some extent even rely upon the narration of an opposing African identity documented in the pass books. In this sense Afrikaners needed Sobukwe to be a black Verwoerd. The threat Sobukwe was perceived to embody was the point of reference for Afrikaner fears, fears that in turn justified Afrikaner claims of sovereignty. Of course it would be a mistake to try to understand Sobukwe's rhetorical power in terms of Afrikaner perceptions alone. If Sobukwe can be characterized as the black Verwoerd beyond the needs of Afrikaners, the power of his rhetoric for Africans would reside in his capacity to forge an identity and claim a source for African sovereignty out of the vulnerability forced upon Africans through the identity and sovereignty Verwoerd forged and the Afrikaners claimed. The point of focus for this contention over persuasive power and vulnerability could be nowhere other than the pass books.

Sobukwe's campaign against the pass laws was a confrontation with the authority of the pass books to assert meaning in the lives of Africans. In this way his campaign was a challenge to the primary instrument of Afrikaner rhetoric. In one of the press releases issued prior to the March 21, 1960, pass law protest, Sobukwe wrote, "I need not list the arguments against the Pass Laws. Their effects are well known. All the evidence of broken homes, tsotsis and gangsterism, the regimentation, oppression and degradation of the African together with straight-jacketing of industry leads to one conclusion, that the pass laws must go. We cannot remain foreigners in our own land." The same press release concludes, "I wish to offer all those non-African individuals and groups who have expressed themselves as bitterly opposed to the Pass Laws an opportunity to participate in this noble campaign. . . . Remember. 'Every man's death diminishes me. For I am involved in mankind" (Pheko, 33). The terms of this justification resonate throughout the liberation struggle and beyond, giving expression to the aspirations for agency and sovereignty that shape post-apartheid South Africa. Sobukwe's challenge is a challenge to the pass books as an instrument of regimentation, a challenge to the imposition of order for which human nature is an obstacle. It is a call for greater expression of human nature. It is a challenge to the divisiveness that purchases the sovereignty of some through the vulnerability of others.

As Sobukwe put it in another release prior to the mass protest, "It must be clearly understood that we are not begging the foreign minorities to treat our people courteously. We are calling on our people to assert their personality. . . . We are not hoping for a change of heart on the part of the Christian oppressor. We are reminding our people that acceptance of any indignity, any insult, any humiliation, is acceptance of inferiority. They must first think of themselves as men and women before they can demand to be treated as such. . . . once the mind is free, once White supremacy has become mentally untenable to our people, it will become physically untenable too—and will go" (Pheko, 28). Here Sobukwe acknowledges the limitations of his persuasiveness. He will not be able to change the minds of Afrikaners. He also recognizes the power of his rhetoric, a power greater than that held by the pass books for which people died. The power of his persuasion is its capacity to encourage Africans to assert themselves, to encourage them to see that they are not inferior, that the pass books do not define who they are, that they too have a sovereign capacity to act.

As the "black Verwoerd," as someone who could inspire Africans to assert their personality, Sobukwe would be most immediately threatening because he could organize the majority African population to action much as Verwoerd had organized the Afrikaners into political power. Since Africans are the majority population, Sobukwe's threat could simply be a matter of his being African, which tells us little of the distinct power of his persuasiveness. Any rhetoric appealing to Africans by attacking the degradations of the pass books would be both threatening to the Afrikaner government and appealing to Africans. That Sobukwe did inspire thousands to march on police stations across South Africa and insist on arrest for violating the pass laws is not necessarily a measure of his persuasiveness, even though it could well be a testament to the ease of appeal to African frustrations with the pass books. This is a possibility. It could be that Sobukwe did nothing more than tell Africans what they wanted to hear. Mandela took this view when he characterized Sobukwe's broad appeal as merely opportunistic. In his autobiography Mandela largely discounts Sobukwe's instigation of the pass law demonstration as amateurish and opportunistic (238), acknowledging at the same time that the events at Sharpeville changed everything in the struggle against apartheid. According to Mandela, the real rhetorical authority in the struggle against apartheid belonged to Chief Luthuli and the ANC, who encouraged the burning of pass books and organized hundreds of thousands of Africans in mass protests and work stoppages in response to the events at Sharpeville (239). Mandela describes the ANC as the voice of the people not only because its influence reached further but because the ANC had a clearer strategy. Mandela's point is that effective rhetoric has more than mass appeal, it has purpose and provides a direction in its appeal, giving a voice to the experiences of the many.

We could take the view with Mandela that the mass demonstration against the pass laws was nothing more than the result of an easy appeal to a people more than ready for any kind of change. This view understands the relationship between rhetoric and vulnerability as one in which people who are already vulnerable become more vulnerable to bad persuasion. There can be no denying that charismatic speakers throughout history have persuaded large groups of desperate people to agree to and do things they would not otherwise do and which are not in their best interests. If this vulnerability to bad rhetoric explained Sobukwe's persuasiveness, the danger of his rhetoric would be less the threat it posed to Afrikaner sovereignty and more the danger it posed to Africans made vulnerable through apartheid to both the force of pass books and the complaints against the pass books.

But this understanding gives Sobukwe's rhetoric too little credit. In large part this is an understanding of rhetoric still wary along with Plato of the susceptibility of vulnerable people to the persuasiveness of what they want to hear rather than their openness to what they need to hear. Echoes of this understanding ring in Mandela's perception of Luthuli and the ANC as deliberate and Sobukwe as "opportunistic." According to this view Sobukwe's opportunism was that he told already vulnerable and so impressionable people what they wanted to hear without enough regard for what they really needed to hear to successfully defeat apartheid. It is in general an understanding of persuasiveness that distrusts the majority. It is in the specific circumstances in South Africa an understanding in which the issue of apartheid becomes for the majority a simple matter of numbers in which the experiences of race and ethnicity decide in advance what people will say and what will persuade them. There can be no denying that apartheid was a product of racism that worked to isolate people for reasons of race alone. By itself this fact implies that Sobukwe's appeal was nothing more than an appeal to African experiences of the injuries of apartheid. But my claim here is that Sobukwe's rhetoric was more than a crude appeal to African experiences of oppression, and Sobukwe did more than pin his hopes for persuasiveness on the recognition that Africans so outnumbered Afrikaners that refusal to obey the pass laws would paralyze the government. Sobukwe's rhetoric did more than appeal to the humiliation and frustration of Africans harassed by the pass laws. He was appealing for both Africans and Afrikaners to imagine a sense, not allowed under apartheid, of self and other and the relationships of self and other through vulnerability to and sovereignty over rhetoric and violence.

When Sobukwe persuaded thousands of Africans to protest the pass laws and march without pass books on police stations across the country, he did ask already vulnerable Africans to endanger themselves. Sobukwe was fully aware of the possibility of police violence as he planned the protest against the pass laws. In leaflets and press reports leading up to the protests he makes a point again and again of the possibility of police responding violently to the massive numbers of African protestors, so much so that it is tempting to say he all but expected it. At the same time he makes clear that the point of the protests is not to arouse a violent response from police. In a publicity campaign leading up to the march, Sobukwe explained the nonviolent nature of the protests and made clear his directive to the marchers that they were to disperse when asked by police. His message was more than the practical one of setting the rules of conduct; he was also calling into question the nature of the constant threat of police violence itself.

In a letter to the South African chief of police five days before the scheduled march, Sobukwe reiterated the nonviolent nature of the protest. He called on Major-General Rademeyer to give orders to his officers to refrain from the use of force: "I am now writing to you to ask you to instruct the Police to refrain from actions that may lead to violence." In the very next sentence he explains the urgency of his request by calling the motives of individual police officers into question: "It is unfortunately true that many white policemen, brought up in the racist hothouse of South Africa, regard themselves as champions of white supremacy and not as law officers. In the African they see an enemy, a threat, not to 'law and order' but to their privileges as whites" (Pheko, 34). These words are far from conciliatory, and it is difficult to imagine Rademeyer even being open to reading them for what they say about the role of the police in the apartheid state. Sobukwe is asking for a directive to not use force in dealing with the protestors, but he is also accusing the police of being more than willing to use force to protect their privilege. The police are an instrument of violent oppression and cannot see they are the protectors of white privilege rather than upholders of the law. Sobukwe's letter does more than appeal for peace during the protests. It directly challenges the authority of the police. By pointing out the racism of the police, Sobukwe is exposing Rademeyer to his complicity in the illegitimate use of state violence.

Confronting Rademeyer with his racism, Sobukwe demonstrates hardly any persuasive power. It is difficult to imagine Rademeyer giving the claims in the letter any careful consideration. It is also difficult to say whether Sobukwe really expected his request to be honored at all. His reiteration of the same point suggests otherwise. As he makes clear in his letter to Rademeyer, the prior actions of the police and the character of its officers leave no doubt how the protestors will be received. They will be met with violence. The letter to Rademeyer, as well as the many other flyers and press releases that communicated the same message in much the same language, can be read not as appeals for nonviolence but as anticipating or even provoking the violence that did occur. Sobukwe knows the likelihood that masses of Africans marching on Afrikaner police officers invites a danger that is all but inevitable. But the violent response of the police is not the point. The point is that Africans, in asserting their authority over their lives, not resort to violence. As he wrote to Rademeyer, "I have given strict instructions, not only to members of my organization but also to the African people in general, that they should not allow themselves to be provoked into violent action by anyone."

The nonviolent intentions of the protest against the pass laws is an effort to create an opening for rhetoric, an appeal for an opportunity—however slim—for interactions that are not so strongly charged with racial disparity. While Sobukwe is appealing to Rademeyer to refrain from violence, his letter suggests his skepticism with the possibility. Violence is the tool of the racist state, a response used by those who cling to their privilege when they feel it is threatened. Sobukwe's persuasive power with the Afrikaners is his ability to get them to see that their violence is an expression of their fear and insecurity regarding the protection of their own privilege. If the police are persuaded to not respond with violence to the protests, then they become aware of the absurdity of their privilege as it is organized through the use of force, and they must engage the Africans. If the police respond with violence, they reveal themselves to be who Sobukwe said they were. Sobukwe makes clear the linking of violence with insecurity in his final instructions to PAC members before the protest: "This is not a game. The white rulers are going to be extremely ruthless. But we must meet their hysterical brutality with calm, iron determination. We are fighting the noblest cause on earth, the liberation of humankind. They are fighting to retrench an outworn, anachronistic, vile system of oppression. We represent progress. They represent decadence" (Pogrund, "Robben Island," 127). At this point Sobukwe appears less like a "black Verwoerd" because his aim is not the imposition of order on humankind but the liberation of humankind from the imposition of order. If his rhetoric is the antithesis of Verwoerd's, then it is in the sense that he exposes Verwoerd's dependence on violence.

At the same time the nonviolence encouraged by Sobukwe on Africans asserts their identities as people with agency beyond the legitimate reach of the state. Where the police may open fire on a crowd out of a racist fear for their own privilege, Sobukwe is clear that it becomes a matter of pride for Africans to assert their autonomy nonviolently. In a press release he explains, "The African people do not need to be controlled. They can control themselves." He goes on, "If the African people are asked to disperse, they will do so in an orderly manner and quietly. They have instructions from me to do so. But we will not run away! If the other side so desires, we will provide them with an opportunity to demonstrate to the world how brutal they can be. We are ready to die for our cause; we are not yet ready to kill for it" (Pheko, 33). The point of the protests is to demonstrate to the Afrikaners that the Africans are people who can and do understand the meaning of law and order. The point is to demonstrate the degree to which the Afrikaners in their quick appeals to violence have forgotten what is just and have organized an unjust state. The point is to demonstrate the illegitimacy of divisiveness. In news releases preceding the launch of the March 21, 1960, positive action campaign against the pass laws, Sobukwe concluded with a call to non-Africans opposed to the pass laws to join the campaign by extending the appeal to nonviolence.

In light of the violent aftermath of the pass law demonstration, the threat of Sobukwe's persuasiveness can be seen as more than his ability to organize mass protest. The power of his rhetoric was more than the power to give the African people a message that would turn their attention toward their own interests and away from the interests of the state. Sharpeville had changed everything in South Africa. His persuasiveness initiated events that escalated the violence in South Africa. He had churned up the issue of the relationship between rhetoric and violence. He had shown that violence is a way for people who fear for their vulnerability to force others to become even more vulnerable. Sobukwe offered the possibility that vulnerability, like sovereignty, is shared by all because everyone is connected to everyone else in humankind.

It would be easy to understand Sobukwe's detention as one small part of the apartheid government's strategy to disrupt anti-apartheid struggle by disorganizing the leadership. No doubt silencing Sobukwe was part of the effort to violently impose an apartheid will and silence voices of dissent. The particular case of Sobukwe also betrays the National Party (NP) understanding of the interweaving of authority, identity, and persuasiveness. Isolation of Sobukwe sets into motion events which unravel the NP understanding of authority, identity, and persuasiveness upon which its own rhetorical sovereignty rested. The desire to detain Sobukwe out of fear of his persuasiveness betrays the realization among Afrikaners that their rhetoric of separation is not persuasive at all. It might be that apartheid leaders such as Vorster simply saw Sobukwe as a "black Verwoerd," as someone who could appeal to Africans the same way Verwoerd appealed to Afrikaners. The fear of Sobukwe in this instance would be no more than an expression of an insecurity experienced by some members of the Afrikaner minority that persuasiveness is acutely color conscious. It is the fear that giving the African majority a voice could and would simply reverse the racial hierarchy.

My claim has been that the fear in the apartheid government of someone with persuasive power who can mobilize the majority against the ruling minority is a fear projected onto Sobukwe's rhetoric from the racialist rhetoric underlying apartheid. While Sobukwe did support the provocative call of "Africa for Africans," he did not insist on race as a qualification for Africanness. Sobukwe's rhetoric was aimed at calling into question the racialist rhetoric of apartheid. To characterize Sobukwe as the "Black Verwoerd" would be to accept the racialist and racist rhetoric of apartheid. According to this rhetoric Sobukwe's words give expression to a collective identity of Africanness that defines itself against whiteness or Europeanness. Such characterizations miss the point. More was at stake in Sobukwe's challenge to the pass laws and his claim of Africa for Africans. In testimony he gave during his trial Sobukwe answered questions following up on his views on the Freedom Charter: "South Africa belongs to all who live in it and as I have already pointed out, our contention is that South Africa is an integral part of the Continent of Africa which historically and geographically belongs to the African people" (Pheko, 58). For Sobukwe the idea of Africa for Africans was not racialist. As he put it, "We aim, politically, at government of the Africans by the Africans for the Africans, with everybody who owes his only loyalty to Africa and who is prepared to accept democratic rule of an African majority being regarded as an African. We guarantee no minority rights, because we think in terms of individuals, not groups" (Pheko, 180). Bound to the land, Africans are bound to each other. They share sovereignty over themselves as well as their vulnerabilities to each other and to democratic rule.

So Sobukwe can appeal to non-Africans to join the campaign against the pass laws at the same time that the campaign does not turn on or even require the cooperation of whites. It is a campaign of self-assertion but not for that a campaign of individualism. As he testified in his trial in response to the question of how many races reside in the continent of Africa, "There is only one race, the human race." He elaborated his non-racialist thinking in response to a question about his secession from the ANC: "the African National Congress at that stage, having adopted a program known as the Freedom Charter stood for what is known as multi-racialism which we have condemned because we say that multi-racialism simply means transfer of the prejudices and bigotry that applies in the present society to a new society" (Pheko, 57). Sobukwe's theoretical position on race is complicated by the historical experience of race on the African continent. Making reference to a slave and his master, Sobukwe pointed out that the two "could not be brothers," a statement that can be taken a number of ways. It could be taken as refusing any potential future bond of brotherhood between black and white on the continent. In the context of Sobukwe's other comments about the Freedom Charter, this interpretation is inconsistent. The refusal of brotherhood rests with those who would resort to violence to secure protection for themselves. A reception of Sobukwe's statement more consistent with his other testimony would be that the persistence of the categories of master and slave prevent establishing the bonds of brotherhood. Not until Africans refuse to accept the subordinate role, not until they decolonize their minds through such efforts as the status campaign, and assert themselves as sovereign agents through such efforts as the positive action campaign, can brotherhood become possible on the continent. In an interview with Fran Buntman, Johnson Mlambo—a former Robben Island prisoner—said that the second PAC president, Zephania Mothopeng, reminded people that Sobukwe believed that "in the new Africa there would be no reason why a predominantly black electorate cannot even have a white person representing them in parliament because color will be of no consequence" (quoted in Buntman, *Robben Island*, 94).

More was involved then in the recognition of Sobukwe's persuasiveness than a crude awareness that his words appealed to the majority black population the same way Verwoerd's words appealed to the minority Afrikaner population. Sobukwe's call of "Africa for Africans" was more than a rallying cry for the majority race to take back its country and assert itself over the minority race. If this were all it was, Sobukwe could fairly be called a "black Verwoerd." His rhetoric would most certainly be threatening to a minority racial group bent on retaining its control over the government, but then his rhetoric would not be an argument against apartheid at all. In fact it would be nothing more than an argument for apartheid with different leaders. Sobukwe's persuasiveness, however, was far more dangerous because it was far more radical. He was more than the "black Verwoerd." Sobukwe's was an anti-apartheid rhetoric. His rhetoric was dangerous to the apartheid government, and so he had to be silenced because of the threat that he could persuade people, black as well as white, that the ideas of racial separation upon which the NP built a society were fundamentally flawed, and the flaw was in the way that rhetoric managed Afrikaner insecurities.

The comparison of Verwoerd and Sobukwe is indicative of the negotiation of vulnerability that connects the rhetoric of the two. Persuasiveness is about more than mere numbers. It is about the power of appeals to vulnerability and through those appeals the making physically real of vulnerability. The apartheid desire expressed in the silencing of Sobukwe is a desire to fashion a rhetoric to remove white South Africans from vulnerability and contingency. It is a desire for stability and certainty, a desire for sovereignty that appeals when necessary to violence and that undermines democracy. As the events of Sharpeville revealed, the rhetoric of sovereignty as configured by apartheid only ended by making everyone less secure and more vulnerable. Sobukwe's challenge, the challenge of his rhetoric, was to show that paths of human development within civil society could follow persuasion in a different direction, away from an imposition of order aspiring for security through control, by embracing vulnerability instead of insisting on sovereignty, by choosing contingency and equivocation over certainty.

Chapter 4

ON THE FRAGILE MEMORIES
OF ROBBEN ISLAND

Today visitors to Robben Island can see the small house where Robert Sobukwe was held in isolation from 1963 to 1969 to contain his persuasive power and to keep him from organizing resistance to apartheid. Guided tours take hundreds of visitors daily through the buildings and across the grounds of the island, stopping for a few minutes in front of Sobukwe's house while a tour guide tells the story of Sobukwe's isolation. The guide describes briefly the interior of the small cottage, tells how Sobukwe spent his days, and recounts how the other political prisoners would catch sight of him as they were marched from the cell blocks past his house to work in the rock quarry. As Nelson Mandela recounted in his autobiography, "we were able to get a glimpse of him in his garden, but that was all" (405). It may not sound like much, but simply catching sight of Sobukwe was enough to inspire some of the political prisoners walking past his cottage on their way to work in the quarry to raise their fists in either the ANC or PAC salutes. Sobukwe would acknowledge the prisoners as they were marched down the road past his house by picking up a handful of soil and letting the sand sift through his fingers, sending the message to the other prisoners that they were children of Africa and "sons of the soil." As former Robben Island prisoner Hamilton Keke explained, "It was a privilege to see the greatest politician in Azania in the flesh" (Pogrund, "Sobukwe," 191). Another former political prisoner, D. M. Zwelonke, put it this way in 1968: "Every time our span of twenty approached that place on our way to work an explicable feeling of joy had filled our hearts: anxiety and worry was banished; suffering and

hunger, forgotten; regret and self-pity condemned as traitors to our cause. . . .
We felt re-vitalised and re-dedicated because no one occupied that house other
than he the most loved by his followers, Robert Mangaliso Sobukwe" (Pogrund,
"Sobukwe," 192).

Sitting in the old tour bus on the road to the quarry, staring out the right
side windows at the fenced-in stone structure, listening to the guide say again
what he has said so many times before, visitors to the island can only imagine catching a glimpse of the man in his isolation. They can only imagine the
anguished monotony of Sobukwe's prison life and the uplifting sight of the man
who would not compromise his resistance to apartheid. All the words written
and spoken about Sobukwe do not seem to adequately express to us today the
experience of his imprisonment or the impact on the other prisoners of seeing
him in his garden. Yet South Africans today recognize and honor his contribution to the liberation struggle and are keen on recalling his legacy to themselves.
This desire to recall was given fullest expression thirty years after Sobukwe's
death from lung cancer. To mark the anniversary, the greater St. Lucia Park,
South Africa's first World Heritage Site, was renamed iSimangaliso, to honor
Sobukwe (*The Mercury,* Nov. 7, 2007). The spirit of the many articles and edi-
torials honoring him in the popular press that year was best captured in Sipho
Seepe's article in the *Pretoria News,* "our future needs this past hero" (Feb. 28,
2008).

Sitting in the tour bus on Robben Island, looking at the small house, strain-
ing to see something that will betray the past, visitors are invited by the tour
guide to open themselves to the place and its history, to make themselves vulnerable to a narrative that secures the meaning of this place in the present of their
lives and for the future of South Africa. Without that narrative, the small stone
cottage appears to be a structure like any other; it does not by itself make known
its place in the present. The uses to which it was put are neither inscribed on
nor currently discernible from its surface. Visitors cannot see without being told
that before it became Sobukwe's prison the building had been part of a colored
school built some time after 1936. Visitors cannot discern without being told
that white warders, or prison guards, were used exclusively to guard Sobukwe
for fear he might turn his captors to his cause. Visitors can see no tangible trace
of any of this. They must be told it. As with any artifact, the tiny compound
does not reveal its past except through the words with which guides attempt to
narrate it. In those accounts of courage and resistance, Sobukwe's house is also
a place through which vulnerability is narrated.

Descriptions of Sobukwe's isolation in the cottage on the far side of Robben Island cannot but tell the tale of Afrikaner fear, a story intertwining bigotry

with insecurity. Descriptions of Sobukwe's isolation also tell the story of Sobukwe's vulnerability to the brute force of the government, despite his refusal to recognize its authority over him. Even after his release from prison, the apartheid government kept Sobukwe isolated. Fearful of the psychological impact of Sobukwe's years of isolation, the government removed him after his release to house arrest in Kimberley, a town where he lived his final years far removed from his birthplace of Graaff-Reinet. Sobukwe's cottage on Robben Island is available for expressing these narratives of intertwined vulnerabilities, narratives that tell a story larger than the building itself, narratives the space neither contains nor reveals through its appearance. A place through which competing and multiple vulnerabilities can be narrated, Sobukwe's house on Robben Island is a metonym for the island itself. Like Sobukwe's house, Robben Island does not reveal itself through its geography. The island must be recalled in the words spoken and written about it. A place through which vulnerabilities can be narrated, the island is in turn a metonym for narratively interweaving the cruelties of apartheid with the ambitions for democracy.

Even in 1961, when the South African government designated Robben Island a prison for enemies of the state, government officials were sensitive to the fact that talk of the island exposed them to challenges to apartheid policy. For example, during the apartheid years foreign dignitaries visiting Cape Town were often brought by government officials to the top of Table Mountain to take in the views of Table Bay. Instead of staying focused on the vista, their attention would invariably turn to conditions on Robben Island, which sits in the bay approximately twelve kilometers offshore. Niel Barnard, former head of the South African National Intelligence Service, explained in an interview: "it was incredibly interesting to see the moment they are on top of Table Mountain they would situate them in such a way that when photos are being taken Robben Island would be in the background. . . . You could've imagined then, we then . . . would start discussing . . . this bloody Robben Island—you must understand that this is not the right way [to conduct diplomacy]" (Buntman, "Robben Island," 311). For Afrikaners the island was a sore spot, a point of embarrassment regarding the enforcement of apartheid at the same time that it was a geographic fulfillment of that policy. And so they were loath to talk about the island as such talk exposed them to questions for which they could provide no satisfactory answers.

During apartheid Robben Island was also a place the vast majority of South Africans had only heard about. It was a place so horrible to contemplate that people were afraid to speak its name, as though somehow uttering the words would bring on its own anguish. As Robben Island archivist Neo Lekgotla laga

Ramoupi has put it, "From a very, very early age, growing up in the 1970s, I was frightened to mention the place *Robben Island*. Because it was narrated to us as this mysterious location, so far away from us, in the middle of the sea, where Robert Sobukwe and Nelson Mandela were imprisoned for life. At that time to us in the townships of South Africa Robben Island was a myth." More myth than reality, Robben Island was known only through the tales told about it, tales about a frightening political prison that reached far beyond the imaginations of children growing up in the townships. Narratives of Robben Island came to stand for the evils of apartheid in the international community as well. ANC President Oliver Tambo captured the rhetorical power of the island in 1980 in a speech he made while accepting the Jawaharlal Nehru Award for International Understanding on behalf of Nelson Mandela, who was still being held prisoner on the island. Tambo observed: "The tragedy of Africa, in racial and political terms is concentrated in the southern tip of the continent—in South Africa, Namibia, and, in a special sense, Robben Island" (199).

Detaining senior leaders of PAC and ANC off the mainland of South Africa, as Tambo remarked, turned attention from the racial politics of apartheid onto Robben Island itself. Imprisoning Mandela and Sobukwe and many other anti-apartheid activists on the island may have effectively disrupted the organization of the liberation struggle, but it also had the effect of directing attention to the place of Robben Island, giving it symbolic weight and rhetorical authority as a geographic point of resistance to apartheid. As Naledi Tsiki explained, "we grew up in the '70s. . . . And we began to read, or to even hear whispers, and the whispers were Nelson Mandela, the man on Robben Island. What is Robben Island? Robben Island is a jail where they keep people who don't like to be pushed around by white people" (Buntman, "Robben Island," 240).

For Africans, Robben Island was the geographic manifestation of apartheid and as such a place to be both feared and hated. They were afraid to talk about a place that invoked for many the insecurity of their lives. People in the townships had no choice, as Ramoupi put it; they understood themselves, they comprehended their own lives, in terms of an ever-present threat of punishment, a threat given added force by expression through the narratives of Robben Island. At the same time the island expressed more than the fear and frustration of Africans living under apartheid. It expressed as well the hopes of those like Tambo who wanted to expose the illegitimacy of apartheid. Despite—or perhaps even because of—use of the island as the place where the apartheid government put those who "don't like to be pushed around by white people," association of the island prison with state power generated an excess of talk about vulnerability within the country and throughout the international community, talk that official narratives could not contain. Continued talk of the island among those Africans living in the townships as well as internationally among diplomats and activists only broadened and deepened the infusion of the narratives into racial experience and political struggle. The name "Robben Island" may have denoted the state's command of force, but for that it also connoted the people's resistance to state-sanctioned violence.

As the apartheid years fade further into the past, the question remains, how do South Africans continue to talk about Robben Island? How do they talk about a place seemingly so overdetermined by the depth of its past and a breadth of narratives that they can imagine saying little else that matters? It is not enough to acknowledge and accept what has already been said. It is not a question of whether South Africans can talk about Robben Island, because they must continue to talk about it, for it is only through their words that they open themselves to its meaning and in so doing make themselves vulnerable to what its physical presence means for how they want to live their lives. At the same time that talk about the island perpetuates its place in their lives, it is only through their words that they free themselves from the grip of the island's history and realize their democratic sovereignty. The island is no longer a mysterious place out of reach on the horizon where people like Sobukwe are sent to be silenced. The island is now a place where people can go and hear and see and experience for themselves the prison where the apartheid government put those who "don't like to be pushed around by white people." Opening Robben Island to tourists signals a commitment to the island being more than a place where South Africans locate the tragedies of apartheid, more than a place where they make the past inaccessible in order to isolate themselves from their history. The island is instead a place where people can come to continue to narrate the present experience of and future hope for democratic South Africa. The question is, how is it to be done? How should South Africans express to themselves and others the power such places have in forming the present without appeal to an inevitability that manages nothing more than explaining those places away? How do they say to themselves and others that the struggle against apartheid could have turned out otherwise while they are explaining why it matters that it turned out as it did? What words will prove adequate to express South Africa's present openness to such a horrible past?

It is not simply a matter of what can be said but also of who gets to say. The question of who has the right and responsibility to give account of the history of Robben Island was at the heart of the assertion of former prisoners that it is they who have a special claim to tell the island's story. Because they experienced first-hand the degradations and horrors of prison life, they claim for themselves a privileged position from which to tell us the truth of the island's past. It is a claim no one can dispute. The truth these men can tell no doubt must be told in the way only they can tell it if South Africans are to understand the past and explain their relationship to it. But as South Africans are aware, truth alone does not lead to reconciliation. The truth of Robben Island, that it was a place where people were made to suffer, is a truth that needs to be told, but that tale of vulnerability to suffering told by those who suffered is by itself not enough to inspire collective openness to a democratic will. The challenge is to tell the truth in a way that inspires reconciliation rather than retribution.

Today the tales of vulnerability that are meant to inspire are those tales told in the cell blocks on Robben Island by tour guides, former prisoners who describe the horrible conditions and degrading treatment, as when they explain how prisoners were forced to perform the tauza, a movement which required them to strip naked and perform a dance that concluded with bending over to expose their anuses. Taken together with descriptions of Sobukwe's isolation, these accounts of prisoner life on the island are intended to appeal to our sense of decency by asking us to respond with disgust and shame to a past none would choose to repeat. Visitors to the island are in fact assured of their decency and of the decency of South African democracy by tour guides who conclude the tour with words echoing Mandela in his inauguration speech as the first democratically elected president of South Africa, "never again." Giving such assurance requires of Robben Island that it be a place where a past is preserved in stark contrast to the security of the present and our ambitions for the future. The assurance of "never again" requires of Robben Island that South Africans continue to recall it to themselves as once having robbed people of their freedom and their dignity. Such assurance also requires that South Africans persuade themselves Robben Island can never again be that place that makes people vulnerable to the degradations of prejudice. The assurance of "never again" requires then drawing the terms for our sovereignty in the present from accounts of their vulnerability in the past.

Since dedication of Robben Island as a South African National Heritage Site in September 1996, and as a World Heritage Site by UNESCO in December 1999, the South African government has provided guidance for the narration of the island by focusing attention on it as the triumph in Africa of the struggles against racial inequality and for democratic justice. Every year since the Robben Island Museum was opened in January 1997, visitors come to the island to listen to guides give tours of the cells of former prisoners and talk about the liberation struggle. The Robben Island Museum website provides images of the island and of the prison, as well as accounts of the island's history and of current curatorial activities. Memoirs of former prisoners, such as Mandela's *Long Walk to Freedom*, Kathrada's *Letters from Robben Island*, and Dlamini's *Hell-Hole*, provide readers with personal insights into the anti-apartheid struggle. These and other symbolic uses of the island, such as adoption there by the African Commission on Human and People's Rights in February 2002 of the "Guidelines and Measures for the Prohibition and Prevention of Torture, Cruel, Inhuman or Degrading Treatment or Punishment in Africa," otherwise known as the "Robben Island Guidelines," become opportunities for emphasizing not what Tambo rightly saw as the tragedy of Africa but what can now be seen as the commitment to human rights on the African continent. This decision to narrate triumph over tragedy is best justified in the words of former Robben Island prisoner Neville Alexander, who describes the intertwining of past and present, explaining South Africans' need to cultivate a civic discourse of understanding without forgetting, of learning to remember without "constantly rekindling the divisive passions of the past." As Alexander puts it, "Such an approach is the only one which would allow us to look down into the darkness of the well of atrocities of the past and to speculate on their causes at the same time as we haul up the waters of hope for a future of dignity and equality" (117–18).

Rearticulating the cultural and material geographies of Robben Island in order to narrate triumph instead of tragedy is crucial to the larger rhetorical project of democratizing South Africa. Alexander makes clear that to choose hope over bitterness does not mean choosing to forget the pain and suffering experienced by so many. Many South Africans either cannot or do not want to forget the deaths and the suffering. Neither do they as a nation want their memories to embitter them. As a physical space containing within its boundaries the remnants of history, Robben Island becomes a resource for narratives of South Africa's emergence from apartheid, a place for recalling a tragic past out of which was carved the democratic present. Today, Robben Island does more than contain the horrors of apartheid in tours that continue to return us to a dark past. In a very real sense, the democratic triumph of South Africa needs a tragic past to persist, not simply as historical fact, but also as formative influence, as always at work in narratives of how the present came to be as it is. The physical space of Robben Island may no longer house political prisoners, but that space can still hold meanings and memories that call on the rhetorical skill of South Africans, as Alexander says, to continue to haul up the waters of hope for the future from the well of past atrocities.

To narrate a hopeful future out of a violent past requires a rhetorical efficacy distinctly different from the apartheid rhetoric that narrated a racialized social order out of an Afrikaner past of struggle for identity and belonging. The efforts of the apartheid government to silence Sobukwe, for example, turned for their success on a view of rhetoric according to which the only viable messages are direct expressions of sovereign agents. This view of rhetoric is more an ambition than a reality. Sobukwe's persuasive power resided not only in the words he spoke. What made his rhetoric so dangerous to the apartheid government was that he acquired in his isolation in his small cottage on Robben Island an even greater authority. His words could not reach the mainland, but through his isolation and his silence his reputation as a leader grew; he became someone who could and did stand against the injustices of apartheid. What the government did not understand was that isolating the threat of Sobukwe and the other political prisoners on Robben Island only served in the end to make that threat stronger. People in the townships whispered rumors about the place. Imprisoned leaders such as Sobukwe, even though they were silenced, were spoken about and so spoke through the talk about Robben Island. The island itself spoke through the discourses about liberation from colonial rule. As Tambo observed, Robben Island itself focused attention onto the larger tragedies of race and politics in the continent of Africa. As a point of reference for discourse about the tragedies of race in Africa, Robben Island is more than a physical place; it is a rhetorical space, a commonplace for the injustices of apartheid.

A rhetorical space, as Roxanne Mountford has described it, is "the geography of a communicative event" which "may include both the cultural and material arrangement, whether intended or fortuitous, of space." She adds, "rhetorical spaces carry the residue of history upon them, but also, perhaps, something else: a physical representation of relationships and ideas" (42). To characterize Robben Island as a rhetorical space is to emphasize the inextricably intertwined cultural, historical, and material geographies that make it significant as communicative event. As rhetorical space, Robben Island is constantly contested. It is dynamic, with appeals to it and uses of it, such as Tambo's, creating spaces for collective deliberation about what was and what can be the state of race relations in South Africa. We all must remain susceptible to the island's narratives as a rhetorical space that continues to speak the open-endedness of democracy everywhere if we are to engage in the creation and discovery of who we are and who we can be together.

As a rhetorical space, as a nexus of the cultural, historical, and material conditions of apartheid, Robben Island serves as physical representation of racial injustice in Africa as a whole. With the official end of apartheid rule and the election of a democratic government in South Africa, the rhetorical terrain of Robben Island required a rearticulation of the cultural significance of the island prison with its contemporary material reality. Harriet Deacon captures the force of Robben Island as rhetorical space to which we remain inevitably susceptible, observing the open-endedness attending the transition from apartheid to democracy: "Seldom has one small piece of land been so heavily imbued with a symbolism which remains, like understandings of its past and hopes for its future, so deeply contested" (161). As Robben Island archivist Ramoupi put it, reflecting on the place of Robben Island first in apartheid and now in democratic South Africa, "At that time to us in the townships of South Africa Robben Island was a myth. Today it is still a mystified place, to some degree. Thus, in these two senses of the past and present, Robben Island has always engaged us. It was never a choice." There is no choice but to engage Robben Island because there has never been a choice in post-apartheid South Africa but to cultivate from the past the possibilities of the future. At the same time, choices are available and do get made about what narratives of the past to tell and how best to tell them, and in those choices reside choices about what future to have, one of hatred or one of hope.

How then do we decide what to tell of the island's long history? Located twelve kilometers from Cape Town, in Table Bay, Robben Island had been used over the centuries as asylum, leper colony, prison, and sanatorium. During the Second World War, the island was used as a military base. Not until 1960 was it used to house political prisoners of the apartheid government. Yet it is as political prison that most people today invoke Robben Island. This is not simply because its use as political prison is most recent; it is no doubt because, as Tambo's observation suggests, that particular use infused the island with singular symbolic value, setting it within larger historical and geographic narratives of racial politics. Nineteenth-century talk about using the island as a wildlife refuge or potential resort were all but forgotten in the 1960s as the island became home to high-profile political prisoners. In a very real sense, the government decision to collect anti-apartheid leaders together in isolation on the island hastened it becoming a symbol both of apartheid's power and of the resolve of those who struggled against that power. Concentration of well-known political prisoners gave clear expression to the force of apartheid discrimination. Assignment of only white guards, or warders, personalized the discriminatory relationships between apartheid's opponents and its functionaries, which contributed to making Robben Island available for being rewritten as a site of struggle by both opponents and victims of apartheid.

During the apartheid years Robben Island was a myth, a story that communicated the basic experience—the fear and helplessness and humiliation—of racial segregation. The story of the island that circulated among people was, in part, a tale of state power. The apartheid government's use of the island as political prison communicated a commitment to preserving the authority of the National Party and to eliminating opposition to minority white rule in South Africa. Isolating prisoners did more than cut off their contact with anti-apartheid organizations. Detaining senior leaders of PAC and ANC off the mainland, as Tambo remarked, focused attention to the racial politics of apartheid onto Robben Island. Directing attention by appealing to and talking about the island made it a central point of focus for contesting and constructing the past, present, and future of South Africa.

Stories of imprisonment and struggle were more than responses to direct experiences of state power and reached far back into African history. The little that people knew about Robben Island was narrated through experiences of the centuries-old conflict between Europeans and Africans on the African continent. Africans, particularly those from the Western Cape, had been sensitive to the island's meaning and had understood it as an expression of resistance to European imperialism since the Dutch first landed in the seventeenth century. Robben Island had so strong a presence that it was embedded in the language awareness of black South Africans. Nelson Mandela, for example, describes the depth of presence of Robben Island in the Xhosa language:

> *Esiquithini.* At the island. That is how the Xhosa people describe the narrow, windswept outcrop of rock that lies eight miles off the coast of Cape Town. Everyone knows which island you are referring to. I first heard about the island as a child. Robben Island was well known among the Xhosa after Makanna (also known as Nxele), the six foot six inch commander of the Xhosa army in the Fourth Xhosa War, was banished there by the British after leading ten thousand warriors against Grahamstown in 1819. He tried to escape from Robben Island by boat, but drowned before reaching shore. The memory of that loss is woven into the language of my people who speak of a "forlorn hope" by the phrase "*Ukuza kuka Nxele*." (340)

The memory of loss and the language of forlorn hope do more than preserve expression of defeat and desperation; they communicate fortitude. To be vulnerable to the emotional force of the memory and the language is to find a way to be resilient. Makanna is not a defeated leader; he is an icon of unwavering resistance to European domination.

Makanna as cultural icon is captured as well in D. M. Zwelonke's 1973 fictionalization of his own imprisonment on Robben Island. Zwelonke describes how he arrived on the island to find a debate raging among political prisoners about rejecting the Dutch name of the island. He writes, "When I came to the Island I found there was much debate about the Africanisation of the name of the Island, Robben Island. The name finally suggested was Makana Island, in memory of the first political victim of colonialism" (15). Changing the name of the island joined the fate of political prisoners to the haunting memory of Makanna. The change in name also reclaimed an experience of the island as sacred ground for Africans. Zwelonke suggests the galvanizing force of the name change by asking: "What was to be the final fate of these doomed men on this devilish, spookish island where the ghost of Makana is believed to roam and lurk to this day?" Joined to the spirit of Makanna, the answer lies elsewhere than in the power of colonial authority: "Their fate could not be finally settled by the falling of rubber stamps in South African courts, declaring a guilty verdict. It cannot be" (13). Instead, the deaths and suffering of Makanna and other Africans make sense in Zwelonke's narrative as contributions to realizing in some future time the end of colonial rule. Their presence at the island, a place of profound significance in the struggle against white rule, made their participation in the struggle crucially important. Telling the tale of suffering in this way helped to steel the nerve of political prisoners by giving purpose to immediate circumstances beyond their control. Zwelonke writes, "We so much loathed being in the mainland prisons, and dreaded being at the Island. But since we were already convicted, and nothing could alter that fact, let us proceed to the place of the martyrs" (13).

Mandela also makes clear in his autobiography how in his imprisonment he joined his fate to a long tradition of struggle against European domination on the African continent. Mandela explains that Makanna is an "African hero," standing in the tradition of Autshumano, who was imprisoned by the Dutch on Robben Island in 1658. Autshumano and Makanna were important symbols for Mandela as he began his sentence on Robben Island. He steeled his nerves by opening himself to their example. "I took solace in the memory of Autshumano," Mandela writes, "for he is reputed to be the first and only man to ever escape from Robben Island, and he did so by rowing to the mainland in a small boat" (340). The legends of Autshumano and Makanna, each in their small boats, alone yet undeterred, crossing back to the mainland, portend Mandela's individual struggle to return from imprisonment and bring to conclusion the struggle against apartheid.

The threat of Robben Island may have served the apartheid government's purpose of intimidating the majority non-white population, but, as Mandela and Zwelonke show, the threat was widely turned to the purpose of preserving the island as an inspiration in African languages and histories. Though the threat of imprisonment was intimidating, such threats were conjoined with tales of Makanna and Autshumano and then Sobukwe and Mandela. Taken up into language and lore through examples of African heroes, threats of imprisonment became more than a threat to be feared; they became a reference point for resistance to life under white rule. People managed to counter the National Party's narrative of authority through appeals to the rhetorical space of Robben Island, a space made available more through openness to what was said than through direct experience of what it was.

As Mountford explains, drawing from Susan Ruddick, the cultural dimensions of space form a "social imaginary," a "sense of locations as having hierarchies and forming relationships" (49). The island served as social imaginary for individual South Africans, such as Ramoupi and Tsiki, who understood their own experiences in the larger terms of apartheid race relations. The rhetorical space of Robben Island as prison, as a location enforcing colonial hierarchies and enabling opposition to those hierarchies, lent persuasive authority to those, such as Mandela and Zwelonke, and the many others who occupied that space. Because Robben Island was already available as the place where historic African leaders continued their fight, the political prisoners of apartheid, held there for rejecting white rule, could take on a mythic status themselves, a status that enabled them to use the rhetorical space of the island to carry on the struggle against apartheid.

Since the mid-1960s, South Africans associated Robben Island with Nelson Mandela and other high-ranking ANC officials, including Walter Sisulu and Govan Mbeki. While these leaders were cut off from contact with the mainland, their presence and their status as heroes and martyrs were perpetuated in words. They were remembered in the anti-apartheid struggle through songs, such as "Bahleli Bonke," in which the call and response—"Where are the leaders?" "They are sitting in jail"—names Robben Island, "NonQonQo," both symbol of oppression and beacon of freedom.

In 1962, prior to the Rivonia Trial at which Mandela was sentenced to life in prison, he was tried and convicted of inciting a strike and leaving the country without a passport. At his sentencing, Mandela addressed the court by calling attention to the vulnerabilities out of which he drew his determination, "I am prepared to pay the penalty even though I know how bitter and desperate is the situation of an African in the prisons of this country. I have been in these prisons and I know how gross is the discrimination, even behind the prison wall, against Africans." Mandela then opposed the conditions of prison to the depth of his conviction, "More powerful than my fear of the dreadful conditions to which I might be subjected in prison is my hatred for the dreadful conditions to which my people are subjected outside prison throughout this country" (332).

Mandela's account of his imprisonment on the island was not to appear until many years later, yet narratives of Robben Island conjoining deplorable conditions in prison with conditions of life under apartheid were already in circulation. These narratives exposed people to the horrors of life in ways they could not ignore, galvanizing the message of struggle against apartheid. Narratives available in oral tradition, protest songs, and local lore amplified the popularity of leaders such as Mandela, placing them in an oppositional relationship to the machinery of oppression. Beginning in the 1970s, various memoirs by former political prisoners, each in its own way, brought dread of prison conditions and the dread of conditions in the townships together with resistance to apartheid. As Paul Gready argues, the autobiographies of political prisoners from Robben Island demonstrate the oppositional power of writing which prisoners utilized to reclaim the space of imprisonment from the state-sanctioned narrative of punishment. Robben Island memoirs in particular are exemplary tales of transformation in which "the worst extremes of oppression and defeat can be turned into resistance and victory, to mobilise and inspire struggles for change" (516).

One such memoir is *Hell-Hole: Reminiscences of a Political Prisoner,* written by Moses Dlamini and published in 1984. Dlamini's narrative of his three years on Robben Island is interspersed with recollections of his youth in a black township where the desperation produced by police brutality, segregation, and poverty crushed the will of black South Africans, inspired some to become political activists, and drove others to organize into violent criminal gangs. Stories of his life before imprisonment do not provide Dlamini the relief of recollection or escape into imagination. Instead, the accounts of life in the black townships resonate with his descriptions of the island as a place that intensifies the degradation and violence of apartheid. The arbitrary and sadistic brutality of the warders, or white prison guards, and the self-destructive violence of the Big Fives, a gang of criminal convicts complicit in the brutal treatment of political prisoners, are presented as intensely focused depredations of an apartheid system that dehumanizes everyone, black and white, who comes into contact with it. In one account of a day at the quarry, Dlamini recounts how a political prisoner, who refuses to address a warder as "baas," is denied permission to move his bowels. Finally unable to control himself any longer, the prisoner, Richmond, goes off to relieve himself and is immediately assaulted by the warder:

Jan has thrown Richmond to the ground, is beating him and is urging him to rise up and remove his shit. "With your hands," he shouts.
. . .

Look at Teeman. See how he turns his body and swerves to the left. His
sharp eyes see everything that is happening to Richmond. He turns his back
again to face us and his legs go up and down rhythmically. Look at old man
Tolepi the former farmhand, with his thin bow legs. He rushes and stands
opposite Teeman and joins him in the *indlamu* war dance. I'm sure his mind
is not here. . . .

Look at the other warders, Piet, Fourie and the Big Fives. See how they
drive those pushing the wheelbarrows. Bloed kicks Steve Lepee from the
back and Steve stumbles forward the front part of his wheelbarrow hitting
Thomas Motloung on his heel opening a gash. . . .

Look at Teeman and Tolepi—how they now dance *indlamu* facing each
other. Listen to the words of the song of how mama tried to give birth and
the child turned out to be a rogue—a reject of society. "It is I who is the
rogue—because I was born Black. I'm White society's scourge—condemned
to live under harsh prison conditions. And prison is the only place for me
where every day in the morning our only consolation is to sing about
parole." (54–56)

Dlamini's explicit direction to "look" one way and then another forces readers to piece together for themselves a scene of incomprehensible barbarity. We
must make sense of something that makes no sense. Richmond scrambles on
the ground as Jan beats him as Teeman and Tolepi dance as the prisoners labor
as the warders and prison gangs run rampant. All the while, all the prisoners sing their subjectivity as rogues, rejects, and scourges. In this passage and
throughout Dlamini's account, the tragedies of race on the African continent
are narrated in terms of the human cost of an apartheid system which abuses
and degrades all Africans of color, including gang members, whom Dlamini
characterizes as the "wrecks of apartheid," wrecks because they have accepted
the roles assigned them by apartheid. With the hope of receiving table scraps,
they eagerly shine the shoes of warders standing watch over prisoners. Lowering
themselves to the status of animals in relation to the white warders, they do not
rise up out of the violence of apartheid, trapping themselves in an endless cycle
of beating, raping, and killing each other.

Dlamini's narrative gives expression to the unrelenting dehumanization of
violence on Robben Island, that was a violence intended to impose the will of

apartheid on its political opponents. Dlamini speculates in his first days of imprisonment that he "could imagine leaving prison like a vegetable, unable to speak coherently—stuttering or with a slur and fearing any White man I come across. And when someone tells of the struggle for freedom—looking at him in shock and just shaking my head" (33). To not leave the island incoherent or fearful, to not become a wreck of apartheid, required that Dlamini and the other political prisoners maintain their humanity by making themselves invulnerable to their captors. Political prisoners found within themselves an ability to maintain their humanity—to not hail warders as "baas," to not dance the "tauza" for warders—by understanding their struggle for dignity and survival as a continuation of the political struggle against apartheid. In all their actions, in all their encounters with prison officials who coaxed them to relinquish affiliation with the ANC or PAC, political prisoners resisted denouncing their political cause, and so resisted denying their humanity.

Characterization of personal struggle for survival on Robben Island as political struggle for freedom from apartheid was fictionalized by Athol Fugard in his 1973 play, *The Island*. In the play, first performed on July 2, 1973, two Robben Islanders share a cell and prepare to perform a version of *Antigone* before their fellow prisoners. Fugard's play begins powerfully, with the two prisoners, John and Winston, miming futile labor and brutal treatment, then dragging themselves, exhausted and injured, into their cell, where the two discuss the play and John's upcoming release from prison. Throughout their dialogue, they display a range of emotions born of their captivity on the island and their bond to each other, from comfort and closeness to anger and distance. In the closing scene, they perform their version of *Antigone*, which becomes a commentary on their own imprisonment and the apartheid regime. In the play, Antigone is accused and pleads guilty to burying her brother, the "traitor" Polynices. Winston, as Antigone, explains the burial:

> You are only a man, Creon. Even as there are laws made by men, so too there are others that come from God. He watches my soul for a transgression even as your spies hide in the bush at night to see who is transgressing your laws. Guilty against God I will not be for any man on this earth. Even without your law, Creon, and the threat of death to whoever defied it, I know I must die. Because of your law and my defiance, that fate is very near. So much the better. Your threat is nothing to me, Creon. But if I had let my mother's son, a Son of the Land, lie there as food for the carrion fly, Hodoshe, my soul would never have known peace. (76)

"Hodoshe" is the Xhosa word for a dung fly. It is also the name John and Winston give to their white guard, or warder. The name is more than literary flourish. Zwelonke tells as well of how the word was used on Robben Island, "We called our span [work crew] the Hodoshe span. Hodoshe was the name we gave our span warder. It is a Xhosa name for the big green fly that feasts on human feces. Although he knew the nickname, he did not know its meaning" (42). For Zwelonke, the name provides a narrative counter to the warder's authority, expressing contempt for the warders by more accurately naming the warder's status in the eyes of the prisoners. The warder who dehumanizes the prisoners is himself dehumanized by them. The name also makes the imprisoned bodies of the political prisoners into that which the hodoshe feeds on. Such dehumanizing did not only counter the degradations of imprisonment. By means of a renaming that isolated body from spirit, prisoners kept themselves free from becoming wrecks of apartheid and available to identify themselves with the long tradition of Africans imprisoned on the island for their struggles against colonial rule.

In Fugard's play, the Robben Islander version of *Antigone* opposes the Hodoshe to Polynices, who is a Son of the Land, a term used to identify black Africans of political conscience who have not been crushed by apartheid. Again, Zwelonke gives expression to what it means to call someone a Child of the Land. He recalls an incident in which a black African, Bra Blacky—broken by the brutal violence of apartheid, devolved into a vicious bully—accosts a young woman in the crowd at a soccer match. Zwelonke's protagonist, Danny, tries to defend her, "'Bra Blacky, don't worry a daughter of the soil,' I was appealing to his feelings of patriotism, because I had just heard him abusing the whites" (25). Those black Africans hailed as Daughters and Sons of the Soil are joined by a bond of kinship stronger than individual impulse, a bond of spirit more binding than the legal mandates of apartheid.

Robben Island is the feeding ground of Hodoshe, where white rulers try to make Sons of the Land into mere carrion through enforcement of abstract apartheid law, a law which dehumanizes because it invokes categories of race that disregard the character and souls of people, turning them into wrecks of apartheid. To obey such illegitimate laws would be to surrender the heritage that makes one human, to become nothing more than the food of the hodoshe. More is at stake in resistance to apartheid than a rejection of South African law. Yet, as John and Winston show through their play within the play, the formal requirements of law that drive Antigone to her end are powerful. John, as Creon, addresses the audience in pronouncing Antigone's sentence: "There was a law. The law was broken. The law stipulated its penalty. My hands are tied. Take her from where she stands, straight to the Island! There wall her up in a cell for life, with enough food to acquit ourselves of the taint of her blood."

In the play within the play, the island where Antigone is sent is a place where formalities of law are vindicated. It is a prison where formal legal requirements are granted much greater weight, and become much more binding, coercing the complete negation of kinship ties and moral obligations. It is a prison where the law is absurd because it is a place where only the exercise of force legitimates it. Antigone is sent there because she refuses the absurdity, because she accords her blood relations and moral obligations greater regard than she does the law. Creon sends her there because he has no legitimacy himself. His authority is propped up by the existence of the island and the degradation it enacts.

In the final words of the play, Winston, still dressed as Antigone, takes a turn addressing the audience, "Brothers and Sisters of the Land! I go now on my last journey. I must leave the light of day forever, for the Island, strange and cold, to be lost between life and death." Removing his Antigone costume, Winston then addresses the audience as himself, "Gods of our Fathers! My Land! My Home! Time waits no longer. I go now to my living death, because I honoured those things to which honour belongs" (77). With these words, the two men resume their posture as prisoners, as they were at the play's beginning, shackled together, shuffling off to the sound of a siren.

While Dlamini's memoir and Fugard's play both join the struggle for daily survival on the island to the struggle against apartheid, making Robben Island represent the constrained, rule-bound injustices and depraved brutality of white rule, the tragedies they convey evoke in their audiences a sense of horror, even arouse feelings of anger, but they do not encourage the spirit of reconciliation that post-apartheid South Africa needed in order to draw out of a past of despair any hope for the future. For there to be hope for a democratic South Africa, Robben Island must be more than what is expressed in Dlamini's and Fugard's portrayals, more than painful inspiration for personal conviction. Narratives of the island must weave together the strands of commitment to a common good that people of all races can share. Such narratives were created by political prisoners such as Mandela during their many years of captivity on the island, as they managed to formulate strategies for continuing their collective political struggle against apartheid in ways that imagined their conditions of imprisonment as a crucible forming their vision for a democratic South Africa. In *Long Walk to Freedom*, Mandela explains, "In the struggle, Robben Island was known as the University. This is not only because of what we learned from books. . . . Robben Island was known as the University because of what we learned from each other" (467). Robben Island was not simply any university, as Zwelonke characterizes it, the island was also specifically known as Makana University, a name emphasizing education and debate as forms of resistance to racial oppression.

On a personal level, characterizing imprisonment as an education provided hope by giving direction. Robben Islanders made efforts in their talk with each other to prevent the degradation and deprivations of captivity to rob them of their dignity. In this instance, Robben Island figures as a counterpoint for constructing not political resistance but personal resolve. Zwelonke describes the personal need for education: "When your soul is low, sunk to the level of brainwashing through dejection, depression, frustration and despair, that is when the white man gets you. Soon you become a stooge, a pimp, a traitor to your cause" (69). Narration of Robben Island as university became another way to counter the dehumanizing conditions of imprisonment. Commitment to education was resistance to brainwashing and refusal to become a wreck of apartheid. Maintaining clarity of thought and affirmation of purpose required constant effort. Among themselves, the prisoners were challenged to preserve what they saw as the legitimacy of their cause and the integrity of their behavior in everything they did. Removed from participation in the larger struggle, Robben Islanders were forced to focus their efforts on their own survival, turning claims for adequate clothing and food, as well as complaints about difficult conditions and harsh treatment, into participation in the anti-apartheid political struggle.

Representation of Robben Island as university had a larger social function as well. During the 1970s and 1980s, the island was the only place in South Africa where members of anti-apartheid organizations could meet to formulate policy and plan action. Particularly in the 1970s, as younger, less formally educated prisoners came to Robben Island, education in the history of ANC and PAC, as well as discipline in collective social action, became increasingly important. Older, long-time prisoners such as Kathrada, Mandela, Mbeki, and Sisulu provided younger prisoners with a systematic political education. The curriculum consisted of courses in the history of the ANC and the African struggle against white domination. There were also courses in economics and politics. Pedagogy consisted primarily of lectures and question-and-answer sessions. The goal was to provide a kind of intellectual coherence to the anti-apartheid struggle to keep it from disintegrating.

In post-apartheid South Africa the brutality of Robben Island, together with the perseverance of political prisoners held there, offers indeterminate resources. On the one hand, the island can become a monument to the brutality and inhumanity of apartheid. On the other hand, it can become a monument to the spirit and tenacity of the anti-apartheid struggle. A simple choice between these two representations of the island would be both politically unsatisfying and rhetorically incomplete. In post-apartheid South Africa, the truth of Robben Island is told as the influences that inhumanity and tenacity have on each other. The story of spirit and tenacity, of living life on Robben Island according to a higher law, would make little sense without an account of the brutality of apartheid injustice. The story of inhumanity on Robben Island could be told without accounting for the triumph of political prisoners and their struggle against apartheid, but telling the tale in this way would distance the past from the present, by distorting, perhaps even compromising, the narrative of democracy still taking shape in the new South Africa. Without distortion or exclusion, the tales told about Robben Island need to best serve the project of reconciliation and nation-building upon which South Africa has embarked.

Former prisoners took the lead in balancing the need to tell the truth against the need for reconciliation in their reinfusion of life into the rhetorical space of Robben Island. One of the earliest examples is a video, "Robben Island: Our University." Produced in 1988, it is an extended interview with three former Islanders, Neville Alexander, Fikile Bam, and Kwedi Mkalipi. During their interviews, the three give accounts of the deprivations they experienced during their years of imprisonment and isolation. They also make the point of wanting their accounts to contribute to a transcendence of past brutalities. Alexander, Bam, and Mkalipi give an account of the past that aspires to transcendence by emphasizing their efforts to maintain their personal dignity and to create political coalitions, efforts which serve as models for retaining humanity in inhumane conditions. Their words and their resilience aim at inspiring awe and encouraging hope. As Mbulelo Mzamane concludes in his 1989 review of the documentary, "One comes away from the film with the feeling that every man-hour wasted by the continued incarceration of people of such colossal honor, integrity, and ability is an irretrievable loss for the entire nation; that our hope for reconciliation in South Africa lies with the release of all such people . . . and that liberation, when it comes to South Africa, will release energies which, creatively channeled, will make the country one of the leading nations of our planet" (98).

In a similar vein of nation-building, Robben Islander Ahmed Kathrada remarked in his opening address to EsiQithini, a 1993 exhibition about Robben Island held at the South Africa Museum, "If I were to sum up in a few sentences our years in prison, I would say: While we will not forget the brutality of apartheid, we will not want Robben Island to be a monument to our hardship and suffering. We would want Robben Island to be a monument . . . reflecting the triumph of the human spirit against the forces of evil. A triumph of non-racialism over bigotry and intolerance. A triumph of a new South Africa over the old." Many high-profile prisoners such as Alexander and Kathrada provided moving examples of forgiveness. As moving as these examples are, such extremes of forgiveness are so disproportionate as to be unimaginable to South African citizens. Alexander, Bam, Mkalipi, and Kathrada may encourage people who know of Robben Island only through words to see it strictly as a place where dignity triumphed, where current leaders held to the justness of their cause and resisted becoming wrecks of apartheid. But, while former prisoners are able through their narratives to reoccupy the rhetorical space of Robben Island, those narratives do not thereby enable the majority of South Africans who had not suffered directly on the island—but who suffered nonetheless under apartheid—a different entry into the space of the new South Africa. Those who did not experience imprisonment on the island sit on the tour buses that roll past the front of Sobukwe's house not fully able to fathom what it could mean to men like Alexander, Bam, Mkalipi, and Kathrada. The challenge remains to find ways of talking about Robben Island that open people to recognizing and exercising their collective dignity as democratic citizens.

With Mandela's election to the presidency in 1994, the man most immediately associated with Robben Island acquired a status and an opportunity to both remake the image of the island and, in so doing, to generate rhetorical resources for an inclusive civic culture. As someone who had suffered for so long on the island, who had in the minds of the majority of black South Africans personified the integrity and fortitude of the struggle against apartheid, Mandela possessed rhetorical authority and had ample opportunity to refigure the space of Robben Island. One of his first efforts came on a visit to the island in February 1995. During this visit, Mandela placed a few small rocks on the ground at the entrance to the quarry where he worked during his twenty-seven-year captivity. Each of the other former political prisoners visiting on that day followed his lead, adding a stone to the growing pile. Robben Islander Mogaman Levy recounts that Mandela, upon placing the first few stones together, told the other former prisoners, "This is how easily a monument can be built" (quoted in McCaslin). The monument they built—a small pile of rocks and stones—is a testament to reconciliation. According to Robben Islander Laloo Chiba, it is an African tradition to place a stone near where one has spent a night safely, to signal to other travelers that they are approaching a place which is, in fact, safe (Chiba interview). By arranging the stones as they did, the former political prisoners reclaimed the physical space of Robben Island as a stopping point on the road to South African democracy.

The pile of stones signals much more than transformation of the island into a safe haven; it participates in a larger rhetoric of reconciliation by re-articulating cultural associations with the island. Just as association of the island with Makanna defined the struggle against apartheid, the integration of the island into a different folk tradition after apartheid introduced new terms for describing the space. Of course, no one but Mandela could have so effectively initiated the rhetorical remapping of Robben Island. His participation in a much larger network of places, activities, and words has refashioned the island as a national monument and popular tourist destination. But even Mandela could not completely manage the rhetorical space of Robben Island.

In 1997, on Heritage Day—a national day of recognition of South Africa's diversity—President Nelson Mandela gave a speech officially opening the Robben Island Museum. In that speech, he narrated a past of the island that proposes a future for South Africa. Mandela invoked the spirit of Heritage Day as a collective commitment of all peoples of South Africa to "Democracy, Tolerance and Human Rights." Collective commitment to such a future requires orientation to a past out of which such values and the commitment to them arise. Conjoining a past of oppression to a future of inclusion shapes the agenda of justice in terms set by injustice. Righting old wrongs and healing old wounds provides motivation to say, "Never again." Unfortunately, disavowing the past can allow resentments to linger. Disavowal also threatens to limit what can be imagined to nothing more than the righting of a particular wrong. Disavowal freezes the meaning of the past in the present and for the future. The rhetorical challenge of drawing productively on the past is the challenge of thawing dialogue and opening interpretation of what has been to a future we have yet to imagine. As Marc Galanter puts it, "The best we can do is allow ourselves to be sensitized by contemplation of the past to the traces of past wrongs that infect the present according to our own standards" (121). In these terms, the challenge of contemplating the past of Robben Island is to rhetorically reoccupy it, and to be occupied by it, to bring forth through such occupation larger perspectives of dignity, equality, and justice.

Mandela's Heritage Day speech illustrates how complex a task the rhetorical reoccupation of Robben Island is. In his speech, Mandela recognizes how important a task it is, identifying Robben Island as "a vital part of South Africa's collective heritage." He does more than ground a just and inclusive future on an unjust and exclusive past; he invokes the memory of Robben Island to clarify the content of a democratic vision:

The memory of the political prisoners confined on this island and in other prisons, reminds us that these ideals must have concrete content if they are to have real meaning. They must bring secure protection under the law, access to justice, clean water, adequate health-care and shelter. They must entrench the conditions in which one can participate in building our collective democratic future; speak one's own language, have pride in one's culture and one's heritage. In seeking to ground our heritage in these ideals we are striking out in a new direction.

For people to participate in shaping the future, they must understand themselves as enfranchised in the present. A large part of the experience of enfranchisement is visible recognition of a past those people can call their own, that they take pride in, and that they can invoke in their deliberation with others. The past of Robben Island, a past of confinement and deprivation, can and does provide a source of culture and heritage to encourage fair distribution of rights and resources. In the rhetoric of so many former prisoners of Robben Island we find strong justification for claims to never again unfairly limit the access of anyone. But the memory of imprisonment on Robben Island, like the memory of other distortions, can, as Mandela said, "inhibit our children's appreciation of the value and strength of our democracy, of tolerance and of human rights. They demean the victims and warp the minds of the perpetrators."

Distortion is prevented when interpretation of the past is as open to dialogue as the future is to possibility. This does not mean every interpretation of every past is reasonable or acceptable, even as the future demands inclusions of the past. Mandela summarized the point: "When our museums and monuments preserve the whole of our diverse heritage, when they are inviting to the public and interact with the changes all around them, then they will strengthen our attachment to human rights, mutual respect and democracy, and help prevent these ever again being violated." Here the horizon that was opened by acknowledging diverse heritages is bounded by preventing the errors of the past. What democratic South Africa can become now is less specifiable and less inspiring than what was imagined under apartheid, when leaders such as Mandela could use the rhetorical space of the island to give powerful expression to their singular visions of justice. Making real a vision of South Africa articulated through Robben Island as a rhetorical space in history requires opening the vision to broader participation and so to reinterpretation. It requires more arguing about images and symbols, a kind of arguing about representations that always threatens to devolve into triviality.

Participation in the rhetorical reoccupation of Robben Island involves asking questions about how to represent its past in a way that reflects the complexity of its heritage. As Mandela asked in his speech, "How do we look at the histories of different people who lived here, through various ages: lepers, prisoners, jailers all together; leaders of resistance not only from South Africa but from as far a field as Namibia and the Indonesian Archipelago? How do we give expression to these diverse histories as a collective heritage?" Answers to such questions were collected, as Mandela noted, from "200 or more submissions received on the future of the Island," and he promised they would be taken account of in forming the national narrative of Robben Island. Similar questions were asked again at a workshop on "Alternative Truth-Telling," held at the Robben Island Museum in May 2000, where scholars, museum officials, and former island prisoners debated the complexities of questions such as: Which stories should be told from prisoners and from warders? Who could tell those stories? Who should benefit from those tellings? And how should they benefit? These are questions for which there are no final answers. There are only responses appropriate to place and time and circumstance.

Philippe-Joseph Salazar has summarized the post-apartheid rhetorical space of the island in terms of current deliberations about its meaning. He points to the prevalence of accounts such as that of Kathrada and Mandela to note their unremarkable character:

> South Africans see Robben Island as proof that dialogue, debate, deliberation can bring together the Just and the Oppressor and transfigure both. In terms of social deliberation and of society as an argumentative process, the epideictic monophony of apartheid has been replaced by polyphonic rhetoric. The key voices are the people themselves, brought to reconciliation (meaning the reconciliation of differences into a public narrative that adopts variegated forms—from voting to talking about themselves as citizens) and born to arguing of what makes democracy workable: the search for a common denominator. (165)

No doubt Salazar is right. Bringing into productive contact the agents and victims of South African apartheid involves dialogue, debate, and deliberation entered into in a spirit of transfiguration. Yet, while such spirit is available broadly, it is also not shared equally by all South Africans. To foster a spirit of reconciliation requires more than openness and inclusiveness, it requires contextualization and encouragement.

David Fleming has characterized occupation of rhetorical space less as a search for a common denominator and more as a matter of how we encounter others:

> If such discourse requires not just respect for basic intelligibility but also respect for the projects of others, then, as arguers, we would seem to benefit from having frequent formal and informal contact with many others, especially those who hold views different from our own, who demand reasons from us when we advance our arguments, and from whom we demand reasons when they advance their arguments, but who nonetheless share with us the responsibilities of managing a common world, who are, in a sense, our "civic friends," although we may not be intimately connected to them, and we may differ in almost every way from them. (159)

A rhetorical space that provides for and enables discourses across difference is a space that encourages collective commitment to a common good by inculcating deliberative respect through repeated appeals to reliable rhetorical commonplaces. Such commonplaces can become trivial and void. They can also become robust rhetorical spaces like Robben Island, spaces which generate in us commitments and which demand from us respect.

For Robben Island to persist as rhetorical space without becoming commonplace requires a balancing of geographies which preserves tragedies and triumphs without distorting past or present. On the one hand, people need the examples of Alexander, Kathrada, and Mandela. They need these examples of seemingly superhuman forgiveness brought down to human proportion if such rhetorics of reconciliation are to spread. On the other hand, people need meaningful opportunities for contributing to mapping the post-apartheid rhetorical space of Robben Island. They need these opportunities to rise out of the mundane human activities of dialoguing, debating, and deliberating if they are to experience the rhetoric as belonging to their heritage. They need a rhetorical space where exemplary rhetors and everyday rhetorical opportunities coexist. This is a space where the ordinary can become exemplary while the exemplary inspires all people to commit themselves to the rhetorical opportunities in front of them. It is a space where both challenges and opportunities reside in communicative acts of arranging and rearranging and rearranging again the cultural and material geographies that people share.

Chapter 5

NELSON MANDELA'S COMPROMISED GESTURE

In his autobiography, *Long Walk to Freedom*, Nelson Mandela describes how on Friday, June 12, 1964, he and the other Rivonia defendants were taken from their sentencing to life imprisonment on Robben Island. As they were driven in a police van past crowds of supporters who were singing "Nkosi Sikelel' iAfrika," the anthem of the African National Congress (ANC), Mandela and the other prisoners gestured through the window, "We made clenched fists through the bars of the window, hoping the crowd could see us, not knowing if they could" (376). Clenched fists reaching through prison bars, communicating solidarity with the people and an unfailing commitment to the struggle against apartheid, made for a poignant moment and a provocative, uncompromising gesture. The clenched fist.

The gesture of Mandela and his fellow prisoners reaching through prison bars was recalled—and forgotten—a little more than thirty years later in the proposal for a Freedom Monument commemorating the struggle against apartheid. Unveiled in April 1996, two years after Mandela became the first democratically elected president of South Africa, the proposed monument was to be built opposite the Vortrekker Monument—a monolithic memorial to the fateful Afrikaner trek inland from the Cape to escape British rule and settle the rugged interior of South Africa. The Freedom Monument site was to include a struggle museum, forty plaques depicting the liberation struggle, an eternal flame, and a wall with the word "freedom" written across it in one hundred languages. The monument itself was to be a thirty-three-meter bronze cast of

Nelson Mandela's arm and open hand reaching upward through broken prison bars. A cast of the original design had the hand on the raised arm clenched in a fist, but Mandela rejected the fist in favor of the open hand because he thought an open hand better denotes freedom ("Proposed Memorial," *Cape Times*, April 1, 1996).

We can speculate about the reasons Mandela rejected the closed fist in favor of the open hand as a representation of freedom. Perhaps he was concerned about appeasing white South Africans. Perhaps he was conscious of signaling that the struggle for freedom had been won. Perhaps he was deliberately distancing himself as a democratically elected president from his past as an imprisoned dissident. Whatever the reasons for his choice in the commemoration of the Freedom Struggle, we can be certain that—thirty years earlier— his choice of gesturing with a closed fist as he was being taken away to imprisonment on Robben Island signaled his determination to carry on the struggle for freedom. Once the struggle had been won, once he had been elected president of South Africa, it is clear that the opportune moment for the closed fist had passed. Just as he had when he placed the first rock at the entrance to the quarry on Robben Island, Mandela seized the opportunity to narratively manage the relationship between South Africa's apartheid past and its democratic present. Mandela masterfully managed South Africa's vulnerability to its apartheid past through discussion of the Freedom Monument controversy. At stake in the decision about the monument is less the question of spaces and the objects with which we occupy spaces and more the question of how we gesture toward each other—how we appeal to, interact with, and respond to each other—in those spaces. Unfortunately, by focusing on the monument itself as opposed to the gestures it was meant to embody, South Africans missed an opportunity to productively grapple with their shared vulnerabilities to their country's divisive past.

While the idea of a national monument to the struggle against apartheid had broad popular support and public appeal, the Freedom Monument proved too controversial to complete. As Marilyn Martin, director of the South African National Gallery, explained in a letter to the editor of the *Cape Times*, the reason the monument should not be built was because the process for choosing the sculpture and the sculptor were undemocratic, resulting in a design that could not represent the struggle or the people or the nation (*Cape Times*, April 4, 1996). Martin was referring to the fact that the idea for the monument originated with Danie de Jager, a sculptor best known in South Africa for his previous depictions of apartheid leaders such as Hendrik Verwoerd. She was also referencing the financing for the project, fifty million rand, which would have been provided privately by Abe and Solly Krok, millionaire brothers who accumulated their fortunes during apartheid through the sale of skin-lightening products. The brothers were asked to provide funding by Mineral and Energy Minister Pik Botha, who was acting on behalf of de Jager. The private nego- tiations infuriated blacks in South Africa, who found it offensive that de Jager would be commissioned to craft the monument. They felt the opportunity should be given to a black sculptor and that it was wrong to even consider de Jager since he was best known for his representations of the apartheid leaders who had kept Mandela in prison for so long. For his part de Jager considered himself the only one who could create a monument to the freedom struggle because he was the only South African sculptor who had experience sculpting monuments on that scale (Coombes, 22). For their part, whites in South Africa complained that a sculpture of that magnitude would represent nothing more than Mandela's ongoing self-aggrandizement (*Chicago Tribune*, April 7, 1996).

It is easy to imagine, as Martin did, that a more democratic and inclusive design competition would yield a less controversial and more representative memorial. At the same time it is hard to believe controversy regarding the proposal degenerated almost completely into disagreements over inclusion in the design process, despite the obvious importance of concerns over the Krok brothers' motivations, De Jager's reputation as a sculptor of Afrikaner monu- ments, and trepidation about Mandela's self-aggrandizement. No doubt genu- ine inclusion in the rhetorical acts of individually submitting and collectively evaluating and finally deciding the design of a national monument matters in a democracy. But as experience has shown, time and again, an inclusive and transparent process is no guarantee of an acceptably representational design. It is a rare thing for anyone to come up with a design for such an important monument capable of satisfying everyone.

This is not to dismiss concerns over the process for funding the Freedom Monument and selecting its sculptor. It is instead to say it is worth looking more closely at the difference made by the choice of who gets to take part in decisions about how to represent a national past. At different times and under differing circumstances people will express a variety of concerns over the role of individual and private interests in the creation of public works. Again, as the director of the South African National Gallery suggested, concerns about inclusion are more than concerns over who gets to participate. Concerns about participation are inescapably concerns about what in the end gets made into a monument; these are concerns about whether the views presented in the process of creating a memorial get represented in the artifact itself. However common it is for people to express their concerns regarding the final product through their concerns about the production process and who gets to take part in it, such expressions mislead. The conjoining of representation in the process and the representativeness of the product begs the questions of whether and how monuments designed inclusively capture a people's sense of a value such as freedom better than monuments designed without concern for inclusiveness. Most people simply assume that inclusiveness in the design process provides assurance that the resulting monument better reflects a community's sense of things. We can acknowledge that broader inclusion does indeed lead more reliably to decisions expressing the status quo without accepting that the decision of the majority expresses democratic values. In the young democracy of South Africa, debate about the Freedom Monument proposal leaves unquestioned assumptions about positive consequences following from broad participation in talk about representing national events, ideals, and values. Questions in South Africa regarding deciding and representing national memory are conjoined questions of how to give expression to reconciliation with a divisive, racist past in order to forge an inclusive, non-racist future. The question of national symbols—here a monument to freedom, Mandela's hand reaching skyward through broken prison bars—is, as Keyan Tomaselli, Arnold Shepperson, and Alum Mpofu put it, a question of whether those symbols can capture the aspirations for public life of current as well as future generations of South Africans.

Questions of collective aspirations are as difficult to pose as they are to answer because they are rhetorical in the extreme—they are as abstract as they are volatile. People do not necessarily know, or even know necessarily well, just what aspirations they have for a public life shared with others. Nor can they say with any certainty what the aspirations of future generations ought to be. Yet when they are confronted with the images of collective aspiration presented in proposals for national symbols such as the Freedom Monument—an image of an open hand breaking through prison bars—people do have reactions so strong that they appear certain of their convictions. The seeming disparity between uncertainty about abstract notions of aspiration and intensity of response to concrete images derives from the formation of aspirations for a way of civic and political life in awareness of experiences in the world. It is not really a disparity at all; it is the way things are. Because we do in part draw our aspirations from being in our world, interacting with, and responding to the objects with which we populate it, national monuments are important architectural artifacts that provide citizens with opportunities for experiencing, and so acquiring, possible expressions for their civic and political aspirations. This is not to say all citizens experience any given national monument in the same way, for they clearly do not. Such aspirations are as amorphous as they are difficult to capture, in large part because people variously interact with monuments and through those interactions variously respond to what those monuments represent as national symbols. This really is as it should be. National monuments achieve their significance rhetorically, by providing occasion for contemplating and debating responses to symbols with which people identify as much as they differ.

Opportunities for citizens to interact with monuments creates opportunities for experiencing a sense of citizenship and belonging, opportunities for nurturing the values of a democratic culture through interactions with others in public spaces. In South Africa one of the clearest examples is Robben Island, where the narrative assurance of the guided tour—"never again"—contributes to forming and sustaining a democratic culture. Philippe-Joseph Salazar celebrates such opportunities as occasions for South Africans to elaborate for themselves a "common good" they can as a nation both share and take pride in. While debate over the proposed Freedom Monument would appear to be an opportunity for furthering divisiveness as opposed to nurturing commonalities, we need not be critical of Salazar's appeal to a common good to worry that dissatisfaction with the collective expression of that common good will persist among citizens. Dissatisfaction has obvious sources. It is not only that people are more or less capable of contributing to the collective expression of a common good, either through lack of opportunity or facility. It is also that people can feel the compromise required for their contribution to the common good asks too much of them. They can feel they have themselves been compromised.

Another example of commemoration makes the point about compromise explicit. In 2002, citizens of Cape Town observed with ambivalence the 350th anniversary of Dutch Commander Jan Van Riebeeck's landing at the Cape, the initial European incursion in Southern Africa. The ambivalence of the anniversary was captured in an exhibition at the Castle of Good Hope which recalled in words and images the 300th anniversary celebration. The tercentenary of Riebeeck's landing, celebrated in 1952, at the apex of apartheid rule, included reenactments of the Dutch landing, as well as enactments of the "first landings" of other races on the Cape from such places as India, Indonesia, and the Caribbean. Of course, there were no such non-European first landings. The reenactments were apartheid pageantry, an attempt to inscribe a particular version of history—a history without indigenous peoples displaced by Europeans—into the memories of all South Africans.

If Riebeeck's legacy were inscribed only in memories and histories, pageants and celebrations, his narrative presence could be easily rewritten in postapartheid South Africa. Yet Riebeeck persists. Aside from his contributions to the trajectory of European colonization, his presence, as well as his persistence, is written into the very geography of Cape Town itself. His statue dominates the city's old main pier. The Castle of Good Hope, built by Riebeeck between 1666 and 1679, remains a prominent landmark. The Company's Garden, planted by Riebeeck in 1652, lies adjacent to the South African House of Parliament.

With the end of apartheid, Cape Town residents began to challenge Dutch domination of their geography by effacing Riebeeck's persistent presence in the city. Riebeeck's statue was dressed in the cape and hat and white face paint of the Xhosa abakwetha—a newly circumscribed male initiate into adulthood— a gesture humiliating and humbling Dutch pretense to superiority. A plaque which marked the almond hedge planted by Riebeeck to delineate European from African was defaced and, in 2001, removed by the newly formed South African Heritage Resources Agency (SAHRA), a national agency organized in 1999 to identify and maintain for future generations the entire range of South Africa's cultural resources.

As much as statues and plaques bear the brunt of people's anger, precisely because they are tangible markers of contention over national heritage, the simple act of removing them does not erase history from people's memories, from their lives, or from the city spaces they share. The past persists in spaces, in words, and in the active gestures that join the two. While any combination of geographies, gestures, and vocabularies may be available for use, we cannot simply organize our cities and our actions and our words into just any combination. We are bound to work with, and even work through, the city spaces and rhetorical practices into which our lives are thrown. Which is to say, rebuilding Cape Town as a post-apartheid city demands more than either erasing or simply forgetting the past. Cape Town residents are bound to work through the spaces and places into which they are thrown. Visitors to the 2002 exhibition on Riebeeck's legacy were asked to participate in reworking the space of Cape Town by being asked the question, "Do you think that SAHRA should replace the plaque [at Riebeeck's hedge]? If so, what words would you inscribe on a new plaque?"

The question of choosing the right words to mark the hedge challenged visitors to the exhibit, as well as the people of Cape Town, to recall what many would probably just as soon forget, but what they cannot forget. But it is not only that. It is also the challenge of having to put into words what they know all too well in their hearts and minds about the racial geographies of colonialism and apartheid. It is the challenge of finding words to express a collective sense of things that does not yet exist. The question, "what words would you inscribe on a new plaque?" challenges people to find words to do more than remember, to do more than describe the landscape, to do more than pass judgment on the boundaries of Dutch colonialism. The question of choosing words to inscribe a new plaque invokes the broader question of reconciliation faced by South Africans since the end of apartheid rule, questions about how to collectively aspire to make sense of the separation of self and other across boundaries of difference built into the landscape, memorialized in monuments, lived in experience, and expressed in words. Annie Coombes makes the point by arguing that South African aspirations for community are developed through engagement with national symbols inherited (such as Robben Island, Riebeeck's almond hedge, the Vortrekker Monument) and proposed (such as the Freedom Monument). As she puts it, "monuments are animated and reanimated only through performance and that performances or rituals focused around a monument are conjunctural" (12). Debate over the proposed Freedom Monument in particular is for Coombes a telling example of the challenge of forging a new cultural policy and national identity that is more than an expression of the current government's legal requirements for citizenship.

Performance and ritual. What people do matters more for their understandings of themselves as citizens than the descriptions of citizenship given them by law. Citizenship is experienced through action, an embodied activity of being in and moving about in a world filled with other people and many things. Such activity is neither arbitrary nor random: it is purposeful, directed by and toward aspirations, experiences, and memories made present through our physical presence. Although Coombes leaves vague what she means by performance and ritual, I describe the performances and rituals of citizenship as embodied expressions grounding in the gestures with which we—at times tentatively, at other times tenaciously—appeal to each other.

Understanding embodiment and performance through gesture has a long tradition. Gestures of the hand have long been acknowledged as integral to rhetoric, not only as accompaniments to oratorical delivery but as visible expressions of the inner state of our thoughts and feelings, and as such, as effective means for evoking thought and feeling in others. We gesture to express to others the content of our thoughts, as when we form shapes in the air as we speak. Our gestures when they are more or less animated also betray the intensity of our feeling, as when we vigorously shake our fists. We frequently use gestures to invite responses from others as well, as when we motion them toward us. We even use gestures to get others to act, as when we point them away from ourselves.

Francis Bacon captured the common-sense notion of gesture as primitive communication, writing in his *Advancement of Learning*, "As the tongue speaketh to the ear, so the gesture speaketh to the eye" (131). Inspired by Bacon, and drawing on a long tradition of recognizing gesture as more primal than speech, John Bulwer described the natural language of the hand: "being the only speech that is natural to man, it may well be called the tongue and general language of human nature which, without teaching, men in all regions of the habitable world do at the first sight most easily understand" (16). Whether naturally acquired or needing to be learned, gestures "open and unfold the sense of the mind," "gain good will," and engage the "incredible force and variety of the affections" (153). All this is to say that gesture does more than accompany and accent our words. Our language has its origins in gestures. Linguistics research confirms the observation made in the 1730s by William Warburton that spoken language evolved from gestural "languages of action" (Rosenfeld, 38–39).

So it is through gestures that we arouse passions in others, express ourselves, and bring ourselves together into groups and communities. Intimately tied to language, our individual gestures become ours through our interactions with others. Just as we find common definitions for words we use to express ourselves, our individual gestures are recognizable to others because gestures themselves can and do get idealized. Through our gestures we expose ourselves to others just as we open ourselves to them. We touch and are touched. We aspire to the sovereignty of our expression through our vulnerability to the expressions of others.

My concern with gesture as expression, together with my brief review of gesture as communication, is motivated by my interest in the choice of gesture selected for the Freedom Monument. The choice of an open hand that was thought to communicate an aspiration for freedom seems straightforward enough. At the time the design was proposed Mandela had already been president of South Africa for two years. The political struggle had ended, and it was time to continue the work of all South Africans learning to trust each other. What made it particularly apt for that moment is that the open hand is an iconic gesture, one with a history reaching back to the idealized gesture of democratic citizenship which belongs to the Ciceronian orator. The ancient orator's open hand extended to an audience signified an appeal from one sovereign self to a group of sovereign others. The appeal begged an openness to persuasive resources all shared, a physical interaction of fellow citizens bound together not by the logic of a claim but by the social character of a common appeal.

As an iconic gesture the Freedom Monument's open hand reaching skyward is not, of course, the gesture of the ancient orator. For one thing the citizens of South Africa are not a homogeneous class who share equally the sovereignty of a common appeal. In post-apartheid South Africa appeals from one group's sense of the common good are appeals easily perceived by others as asking them to compromise on the aspirations with which they would define democratic citizenship. The idealized gesture of Mandela's open hand reaching through broken prison bars—not the actual gesture of Mandela reaching his clenched fist through a police van window—attempts to ease the feeling of begrudging compromise by appealing to South Africans to respond in kind, to themselves become the kind of citizens who share equally in a common good out of which they find sympathy with each other. The open hand of the monument asks South Africans to model themselves on the idealized gesture, to signal their compromise on divisive issues as they gesture toward each other in the performance of their citizenship. This is not simply a straightforward matter of people adopting the gesture of a monument which is itself the representation of a leader's pose. Since the hand from which the monument was cast is real and the gesture into which it was cast is ideal, questions raised by the proposed monument become questions of the compromises made in the act of making a person's gesture into a monumental symbol, the kinds of compromises reflected in the monument itself, and the extent of compromises meant to be elicited from South Africans who would aspire to perform their citizenship through their contact with the Freedom Monument.

Another way to put it is to say that, whatever the problems of compromise in the design process for the Freedom Monument, the design itself is an expression of compromise—a hand reaching skyward through broken prison bars, an open hand meant to represent an ideal of freedom. But not just any hand, Mandela's hand. The hand of the man who had spent twenty-seven years imprisoned on Robben Island for his role in the struggle against apartheid. The hand of the man who upon his release became the first democratically elected president of post-apartheid South Africa. The hand of the man who had come in so many ways to personify the yearning for freedom and the character of democracy. An open hand, though, not a fist, because Mandela thought a hand would be somehow more representative of the ideal of freedom, freedom as an aspiration, something to gesture toward and reach for.

I do not know whether Mandela in his choice for the Freedom Monument design recalled having reached his clenched fist through the bars of a police van. It is highly unlikely—and it would be odd indeed—if the Freedom Monument design was inspired by that moment in 1964. Yet the clenched fists that reached through those bars did gesture an uncompromising commitment to freedom. In the context of South African history a closed fist reaching through prison bars looks like a resonant symbol with which to commemorate the liberation struggle. In fact Mandela gesturing with raised closed fist—the salute of the ANC—is so ubiquitous an image it is hard to imagine him gesturing with open hand. Perhaps the most famous photograph of Nelson Mandela is the image of him upon his release from prison in February 1990. His expression is jubilant, his hand raised in a clenched fist of both triumph and resolve. He explains the power of that moment in his autobiography. Stepping outside the gates of Vorster prison into a crowd of reporters and supporters, "Reporters started shouting questions; television crews began crowding in; ANC supporters were yelling and cheering. It was a happy, if slightly disorienting chaos. . . . When I was among the crowd I raised my right fist and there was a roar. I had not been able to do that for twenty-seven years and it gave me a surge of strength and joy" (563).

The scene Mandela describes upon his release from prison is a scene of people pressing in—a din of questions and yelling and noise. Sound and sensation sweep him away, penetrating and overwhelming him to the point he raises his hand in a clenched fist. The gesture is almost a reflex, a response to the crowd and the noise and the freedom, a response to feeling the coming twilight of apartheid. An overwhelming sensation that built into an urge, an urge to express something. An overwhelming sensation of joy that drove Mandela's raised fist high into the air for the crowd to see.

Mandela's gesture of saluting with clenched fist—first from the police van, then amid the crowd outside Vorster prison—brackets his imprisonment. Upon his sentencing the fist is a gesture of defiance. Mandela and the other Rivonia defendants signal with their raised fists their collective refusal to suffer their vulnerability to the state's power to imprison them. Upon his release from prison Mandela raises his fist in a gesture of exuberance, his revolutionary resolve renewed as the end of apartheid appeared more and more certain. This time the raised fist was a gesture celebrating victory instead of a gesture confirming resolve. Open to and inspired by the crowd that gathered to witness his release, Mandela thrust his fist into the air, a gesture that continues to resonate in South Africa, a resonance echoed by kwaito artists Prophets of da City, who celebrated Mandela's election as president with the lines, "Africa rejoice. Raise your fist, raise your voice."

The exuberance of gesturing does more than communicate meaning: the gesture is itself meaning. We gesture with our hands often without intending to do so. If we are excited and passionate enough, our gesturing hands can also be used violently. We can even strike each other. We live together on this continuum of embodied expression, from swinging violently, to gesturing for expression, to sculpting idealizations of freedom. Because we can and do express ourselves physically through gesture we are also vulnerable to physical violence. Maurice Merleau-Ponty put it most succinctly: "The gesture does not make me think of anger, it is anger itself" (214). The gesture of anger is anger because it is, as is all gesture, the body physically manifesting experience. As Mandela put it when he explained the spontaneity of his gesturing with closed fist upon his release from prison, he felt himself swept away in the moment. As instinctual as the gesture of raising his fist may have felt to Mandela, that gesture is not for this reason a gesture that is unlearned. To raise a fist in the air, in that place, at that time, is to invoke a history of signifying with our bodies.

Over the course of the twentieth century in particular the raised fist has been a gesture associated with violence that affirms a sense of freedom and solidarity. For European workers prior to the early 1920s, the gesture of the handshake best represented fraternal identifications and the united opposition to oppression. The closed fist was consciously adopted as a symbol of worker solidarity by the international workers movement at the start of the twentieth century. The symbol itself was a formalization of the gesture of the worker's fist raised in protest that emerged in the labor strikes of the 1880s as a "spontaneous gesture of protest, discontent, and readiness to fight" (Korff, 77). Similarly for the German Communist Party between the world wars the gesture of the raised closed fist was consciously adopted as a symbol of solidarity in defiance of an emerging fascism (81). The symbolism of the fist was made iconic through its adoption and dissemination in the graphic design of political propaganda intended to counter the ritualized palm forward salute of the Nazis (Simmons). As a symbol of solidarity and resistance the raised closed fist was readily taken up in other political and social struggles. In the United States, for example, the black-power fist as gesture against racial inequality and for civil rights gained prominence in the 1960s as more radical civil rights leaders became increasingly impatient with the slow progress of the struggle for racial equality. In short, the raised fist as a gesture symbolizes defiance; it signals a pose of insurgency. But it is not for this reason a gesture that signals undemocratic sentiments. The raised fist is a gesture of solidarity. It is the gesture of those people whose rejection of totalitarianism and colonialism was secured through an unwillingness to compromise, an unwillingness to accept the demand for conciliation to universals that exclude. Gesturing discontent and an impatience with not being heard, the closed fist became a gesture of revolution, an expression of inclusion rather than exclusion, a revolutionary gesture of inclusion in anti-fascist, anti-capitalist, and more often than not pro-communist and pro-Marxist movements.

In South Africa the gesture of raised, closed fist has a symbolic value that resonates with themes of revolution and solidarity. The ANC logo is a shield in front of which is a hand clenching a spear and a wheel of about the same size.

The logo was adopted in January 1987 on the seventy-fifth anniversary of the founding of the ANC. The spear and shield "represent the early wars of resistance to colonial rule, the armed struggle of the ANC's former wing, Umkhonto we Sizwe, and the ANC's ongoing struggle against privilege and oppression" (www.anc.org.za). The wheel "is a symbol of the strong non-racial traditions of the ANC," while the "fist holding the spear represents the power of a people united in struggle for freedom and equality." Since 1993 the logo has been added to the center of the black, green, and gold flag of the organization. A fist figures more prominently in the symbolism of another South African political party, the Azanian People's Organization (AZAPO). AZAPO describes the revolutionary symbolism quite matter-of-factly: "a right hand Black clenched fist facing forward with a Red Star imposed on the Wrist on a Gold Background."

I have taken the time to dissociate Mandela's gestures from political symbolism in South Africa and the design of the proposed Freedom Monument to draw attention to the ambivalence of the monumental gesture. The skyward-reaching hand may be recognizable as an iconic gesture, but we need to remind ourselves that, while gesturing is a universal feature of human communication, the iconicity of any given gesture is not. A gesture originates in time, out of being in a moment, the way Mandela's gesture originated in the moment of his release from prison, a moment and a gesture made poignant through their groundedness in particular historical contexts. Gestures always manage this expressive duplicity. On the one hand a gesture is an effort to give external form to feelings that well up from deep inside. On the other hand the iconicity of a gesture has its origins in conventions established through such things as declaration, habit, and custom. Between expressive gestures through which we open ourselves to others and the iconic gestures through which values and understandings are imposed on us, we manage multiple vulnerabilities. We expose ourselves in our exuberance to others, as they expose themselves to us. And we all expose ourselves to claims made on our attention, our concern, and our resources by icons and monuments.

It is a question worth considering whether the decision to use an open hand instead of a closed fist in the design of the Freedom Monument was an attempt to communicate a sense of freedom enlarged beyond the sense of freedom made iconic by the ANC in the struggle against apartheid. It is easy enough to imagine that the open hand was considered a more conciliatory and inclusive gesture. At the same time, the open hand compromised expression of the struggle through which freedom is won. But the choice of gesture did more than compromise the memory of the struggle. My suggestion that it was a compromise to represent freedom through an upward-reaching hand instead of an upward-thrusting fist is also a suggestion that the open hand of the proposed Freedom Monument is less an icon of some common aspiration for freedom and more a refusal to grasp contentious issues that remain divisive in South Africa.

To see how this is so, recall that the closed fist of the ANC salute is a gesture of solidarity and struggle. It is also the gesture most recognizably associated with Mandela. Yet it is the gesture he rejected as not communicating freedom as compellingly as the open hand. The open hand is less specific, more iconically a gesture of inclusion. The open hand is a gesture more removed from actions and so less evocative of specific moments such as Mandela's sentencing to and release from prison. To put it less in terms of iconicity and specificity and more in terms of contingency, the choice of hand over fist in the design of the Freedom Monument gives expression to preference for the certainty of emblematic expressions of generalizability and predictability over expressions of the contingency of embodied gestures that are as subtle as they are spontaneous. The question of whether a fist or an open hand better represents freedom invokes issues of embodied experiences of solidarity and struggle as well as expressions of democratic aspirations. The question of whether freedom is better represented through clenched fist or open hand is the question of whether and how to represent the ideal of freedom as allowing space for disagreements and difference. This is, as I see it, the question South African political cartoonist Zapiro raised in his representation of the Freedom Monument controversy.

Zapiro's response to the controversy over the Freedom Monument, "The Urban Handscape," is a single-panel cartoon dominated on the left by a rendition of the proposed Freedom Monument, a hand reaching skyward through broken prison bars. On its base is inscribed the name of Nelson Mandela. In the center of the urban handscape, slightly further back from the foreground, is a hand clenched in a fist with its forefinger raised. On its base is the name of P. W. Botha. Pieter Willem Botha was elected prime minister of South Africa in 1978 and served as the country's president from 1984 to 1989. During those years he was an unwavering supporter of apartheid, even though such support plunged his country ever further into chaos. It was Botha's successor, F. W. de Klerk, who led the apartheid government to the negotiating table with the ANC. In the Zapiro cartoon the gesture of a raised forefinger recalls a speech to the apartheid government's National Party congress given by Botha on August 15, 1985. In that speech Botha remarked, "I believe that we are today crossing the Rubicon in South Africa," recalling Caesar's fateful decision to take his legions across the Rubicon River in northern Italy and plunge Rome into a disastrous civil war. Invoking the threat of protracted violence, Botha raised his finger in the air and proclaimed, "Don't push us too far" (Moriarty, 19). His finger-waging threat was as much a warning to insurgents as it was an appeal to his party for support.

The final monument in the urban handscape is slightly foreground and to the right of the Botha hand. It is a hand with its middle finger extended, its back toward the Mandela hand as if gesturing to it. On its base is the name of the Inkatha Freedom Party (IFP) leader, Chief Mangosuthu Buthelezi. This gesture does not so much recall a physical gesture ever made in public by Buthelezi as much as it characterizes his increasingly antagonistic relationship with Mandela and the growing tensions between the ANC and the IFP in the transition to a democratic South Africa. Originally a member of the ANC, Buthelezi broke with the party in 1979 after the ANC denounced him for collaborating with the apartheid government and serving as administrator of the Zulu Homeland (Thompson, 249). As chief of a native Homeland, Buthelezi aspired for a post-apartheid South Africa constituted by rather autonomous ethnic states in which he could retain his position and authority. Marginalized from the negotiated settlement between the ANC and the government, Buthelezi and the IFP resorted to more violent measures, often clashing with ANC supporters in the townships surrounding Durban (249–50). To prevent South Africa from devolving into total civil war, the three leaders—Buthelezi, de Klerk, and Mandela—met in Johannesburg with the leaders of other political parties on September 14, 1991, to sign a code of conduct prohibiting the use of intimidation, threat, or violence. Buthelezi brought with him to the ceremonial signing two thousand armed Zulu warriors. After the signing Buthelezi refused to shake the hands of either de Klerk or Mandela. De Klerk was conciliatory, but Mandela was furious and lashed out publicly at de Klerk (Ottaway 166–68). Buthelezi likely did not see his failure to shake the hands of de Klerk and Mandela as an affront. The prominence of the ANC, and its capacity for setting the terms for post-apartheid South Africa, marginalized the IFP ethnic agenda and left Buthelezi feeling snubbed. As he remarked in a speech he gave upon Mandela's release from prison—signaling both the growing tensions and common connections of the ANC and IFP—Buthelezi said, "The ANC must not remain petulant while South Africa burns. . . . Where, Dr. Mandela, I ask, is your hand of friendship?" (Moriarty, 60).

Placing the planned Freedom Monument together with the imagined Botha and Buthelezi monuments, Zapiro's "Urban Handscape" recalls gestures of political aspiration and antagonism familiar to all South Africans. The question raised by Zapiro's cartoon is of the relationship between the performance of those gestures and their permanence or persistence in the South African landscape. Do the different gestures, as Zapiro's cartoon suggests, represent a landscape in which it is impossible for South Africans to approach each other differently? Zapiro's cartoon may resonate with frustrations that South Africans feel in their dealings with each other by referencing common awareness of recent events and violent tensions, but it conveys much more. Of the gestures portrayed on the three monuments, only Botha's was real. He did in the midst of making a speech wag his forefinger as a gesture emphasizing his conviction. Buthelezi may have gained notoriety for his disdain and disregard of the negotiations and later of the South African Truth and Reconciliation Commission, but he never publicly used the gesture of an extended middle finger. This is not to say that the gesture assigned to Buthelezi by Zapiro does not in some sense ring true, for it surely does. It is to say the gesture is nothing more than a characterization of Buthelezi's actions and attitudes.

The Mandela gesture in the "Urban Handscape" may be true to the design of the Freedom Monument; it might even be argued that the gesture in some sense indicates the spirit of the struggle against apartheid, but that does not make the gesture true to any that Mandela himself ever made. Nor does it match the spirit of the gesture with the political symbolism adopted by the ANC. No, the historically true gesture, as well as the ideologically appropriate one, is the raised clenched first chosen but then rejected in the initial design of the monument. At the same time, though, Mandela did approve the open hand for the design of the monument, a gesture of reconciliation through which Mandela appeals to his former enemies for cooperation.

As Zapiro's satire of the Freedom Monument suggests, gesture signifies across the range of individual moment, human character, and national ideal. The urban handscape is a landscape of gestures, both real and imagined. They not only dominate the horizon, they define it. The resistance of the gestures of Buthelezi and Botha memorialize the unified resistance of white Afrikaners and the divisiveness of tribal connections. These are set against an idealized gesture of Mandela reaching for freedom, freedom from the narrow and divisive gestures and rhetorics of racists and tribalists alike. In a generous reading of the cartoon, juxtaposition of open hand to wagging finger to obscene gesture captures what people want to remember as the spirit of compromise that Mandela skillfully nurtured in his leadership of South Africa's transition into democracy. At the same time the urban handscape points out the inaccuracy of memories. The gestures of Buthelezi and Botha are respectively characteristic and actual, while the gesture of Mandela is simply imagined. During the struggle against apartheid upon his release from prison, even after he was elected president, Mandela continued to raise his clenched fist in the ANC salute. Yet, if we imagine a fist in place of the open hand in Zapiro's urban handscape, the resulting image would seem jarringly uncharacteristic of Mandela, even though Mandela's raised fist juxtaposed to Botha's extended forefinger juxtaposed to Buthelezi's raised middle finger might better represent the contentious landscape of South Africa in the waning years of apartheid. While it may be that a raised closed fist might be a more accurate representation of the spirit of the liberation struggle, the juxtaposition of fist to waging forefinger to raised middle finger would not represent the genuine aspirations for a democratic landscape shared by many South Africans.

Moving back from the embodied interactions of living people struggling to communicate with each other to the disembodied representations of meaning, Zapiro's sketch of raised forefinger and raised middle finger prevents a too-easy reduction of the differences that divide South Africans who have no choice but to join together in democratic governance. There is more, then, to iconic gestures real and imagined than the monumentalizing of important national figures and movements. The iconic gestures represented by Zapiro are part of a larger landscape of gesture occupied by all people of South Africa. Any monument to the liberation struggle, to Nelson Mandela, or even to freedom that drew on the open hand could not but be an attempt to insert meaning into an environment in which that meaning did not exist before, to create something that was not there, to embody an aspiration for openness and conciliation in the space all citizens share.

If an open hand is the gesture needed in post-apartheid South Africa because it is the gesture associated with conciliation, then one possible explanation for discomfort with the closed fist says the fist represents a threat of violence. But this explanation only goes so far. The closed fist can certainly be seen as physical threat, and the threat of violence is itself the opposite of freedom. Physical violence is coercion embodied, an unconstrained use of force. Rage. But the closed fist as gesture embodies much more than force, rage, and the threat of violence. At the same time, the violence of striking someone with clenched fist entails much less than a closed fisted gesture represents. An open hand can slap or grab just as easily as a clenched fist can punch. A gesture is much more than a simple physical act, and the representing of that gesture in metal or stone is much more still. How we perceive the articulation of action, gesture, and representation speaks to our understandings of the embodiment of rhetoric, the lived experiencing and expressing of collective aspirations for citizenship and nationhood. The gesture embodies more. Levels of comfort with fist or hand as more or less representative of freedom expresses perceptions about the anxiety of influence of public rhetoric as well as concern over individual autonomy, freedom from coercion, and the role of violence in achieving democracy.

For several years after Mandela's release, throughout the negotiated settlement of the transition to a new government, the open hand of compromise was not always extended. The success of negotiations did not always turn on compromise as much as it was driven by the threat of violence. The year Mandela was released from prison, President de Klerk rescinded the ban on the ANC and other political organizations, making it possible for the government to negotiate peace with the ANC. With the lifting of the ban on anti-apartheid political organizations, violence in South Africa escalated. Protestors took to the streets in anticipation of an end to apartheid rule, and violence spread. The police responded with force, shooting many. As chaos spread, the South African government initiated Operation Iron Fist. Begun on September 15, 1990, Operation Iron Fist called for police to use curfews, vehicles with machine guns, aerial spray dyes, and razor-wire barricades to encircle worker hostels and squatter camps. Twenty-seven townships were placed under emergency rule. By September 19 police contributions to the violence had encouraged many, including Mandela, to call for an inquiry. At the same time the ANC initiated what it called Operation Vula, or "opening," aimed at undermining the authority of the government. More than once between 1990 and 1993 talks broke down as escalating violence and continued bloodshed constantly threatened to undermine trust in the negotiations for a transfer of power.

Ultimately the transition to a multiracial government in South Africa was not won through a gesture of open-handed compromise alone. But neither was it won through a romanticized gesture of closed-fisted solidarity. The animosity and violence that accompanied the transition were part of the process, at times hindering it and at other times encouraging it. As an emblematic gesture the fist may remind too many people of the struggle that divided them for so long. Yet the open hand as an emblem of the struggle for freedom and the discovery of unity has too little resonance; it does not speak to the struggle people experienced in their lives. The open hand is not in this instance an embodiment of rhetoric.

In 2002, six years after the unveiling of the Freedom Monument proposal, the South African government offered support to another private plan to build a monument to Nelson Mandela, this one in Port Elizabeth. This monument, a statue of Mandela over 110 meters high—taller than the Statue of Liberty—also originally had Mandela's arm raised in a clenched fist. A second design, one with his arm raised in an open hand reaching skyward, succeeded the first, "due to discomfort in some quarters with the fist symbol" ("Giant Mandela Statue Planned"). This project too was initiated by a private investor, advertising executive Kenny McDonald, who envisioned the statue as a key to the development of the tourist industry in Port Elizabeth. Like the Freedom Monument, this design was rejected in favor of soliciting a design through the more democratic process of open competition.

While neither the Freedom Monument nor the Mandela "Freedom Statue" was ever built, a monument was eventually approved for Port Elizabeth. The winning design in the competition was not a representation of bodies. It was a winding 122-meter Freedom Tower consisting of a spiral series of stairs meant to lead visitors along Mandela's and South Africa's long journey to democracy. At the top of the structure visitors emerge onto an open-air observatory. As the judges of the design competition observed, "The ascent from darkness to light will be immediately understandable. . . . The layered progression of the freedom struggle will be strongly represented" ("A Freedom Tower for Mandela"). In the end the Freedom Tower is perhaps the best embodiment of a democratic rhetoric because it does ask for our vulnerability. Rather than representing the gestures of bodies as the Freedom Monument did, the winning design engages the bodies of visitors, inviting them to take a journey, to walk both ways to the difficulties of embodying democracy, from darkness to light and back again.

Chapter 6

DESMOND TUTU'S
EVEN-HANDEDNESS

If the gesture of conciliation—the open hand extended to another—belonged to anyone in the struggle for democracy in South Africa, it was not Nelson Mandela. It was Archbishop Desmond Tutu. From 1967 as chaplain at University of Fort Hare, to bishop of Lesotho in 1976, to secretary-general of the South African Council of Churches in 1978, Tutu consistently persisted in his appeal for an end to apartheid and for reconciliation between the apartheid government and its opposition. In 1986 when he became the first African archbishop of the Anglican Church of South Africa, Tutu continued to advocate for reconciliation, all the while denouncing the injustices of apartheid and criticizing the violence of apartheid's opponents.

As the chairperson of South Africa's Truth and Reconciliation Commission (TRC), Tutu extended his hand and opened his arms in a public gesture of reconciliation, inviting the participation of all South Africans. Some, however, rejected his gesture. There were the Afrikaners suspicious of Tutu's gesture of compromise, perceiving him to be nothing more than a functionary of the African National Congress (ANC). They worried that the goal of the TRC was to do no more than blame the previous government and praise the new government. They feared a victor's vengeance. There were Africans critical of Tutu as well. They believed reconciling with Afrikaners would do nothing but compromise the success of the struggle against the injustices of apartheid. However much he may have compromised, Tutu did not understand the choice between forgiveness and justice as a choice between incompatible options. Instead he saw his

role as doing more than promoting forgiveness at the expense of exacting justice. If anything, Tutu's conciliatory rhetoric aimed at persuading those Afrikaners and Africans suspicious of each other and distrustful of reconciliation that
they could come to share a common language of cooperation. With distrust and
suspicion close beneath the surface of every decision—the design of the Freedom Monument being only one example—the challenge Tutu faced was how to
neutralize the dispositions toward others that hindered communication. Being
neutral, being careful to appear dispassionate in one's words, is certainly a rhetorical strategy for overcoming distrust and suspicion. Tutu, however, decided
a rhetoric of neutrality was inadequate to the task of establishing a language of
trust and cooperation in South Africa.

In his foreword to the final report of the TRC, Tutu characterizes his gesture
of conciliation not as open-handed, not as an unconditional invitation to cooperation, but as even-handed, a gesture balancing his condemnation of apartheid
with his willingness to consider the motives of apartheid's administrators. He
puts it this way: "I cannot, however, be asked to be neutral about apartheid. It
is an intrinsically evil system. But I *am* even-handed in that I will let an apartheid supporter tell me what he or she sincerely believed moved him or her, and
what his or her insights and perspectives were; and I will take these seriously
into account in making my findings" (1: 13). Tutu is clear: even-handedness is
not neutrality. It is also not partisanship. To be even-handed does not require
accepting the legitimacy either of apartheid or of the actions of those who perpetuated the system and profited from it. Neither does it require accepting as
legitimate any acts committed in the name of overthrowing the apartheid government. To be even-handed does, however, require a willingness to take seriously people's accounts of their own actions, a willingness to be persuaded of
people's motivations for their actions without thereby excusing or denying the
consequences of those actions. A rhetoric of even-handedness allows for people
to explain their actions by listening to the accounts they give of their motives. It
allows for people to have an opportunity to explain why they did what they did,
without such accounting excusing what has been done. To listen even-handedly
to the accounts people give of themselves and their actions is to remain firm in
the view that neither sincerity of motive nor strength of conviction makes an
unjust act just. Neither, then, does the rightness of the cause give moral privilege
to immoral actions. Tutu is clear about this as well: the justness of the struggle
against apartheid did not make any actions undertaken in the name of liberation into just acts.

Even-handedness demands recognizing that human rights abuses are human
rights abuses no matter who commits them, no matter their reasons. In this way

even-handedness is uncompromising about what is and is not just. Refusing to compromise on what is just would seem to threaten to make even-handedness unforgiving. Refusing to compromise on the issue of amnesty for the injustices of apartheid would seem to confirm Afrikaner fears that claims about forgiveness and reconciliation are empty words not to be trusted—but not for Tutu. In the accounts people give of themselves, their motives, insight, and perspective do matter because those expressions of personal experience provide grounds for forgiveness. In the accounts people gave before the TRC, motive, insight, and perspective mattered not because they provided reasons to excuse human rights abuses or the injustices of apartheid but because these personal expressions give us pause to comprehend human actions in their fullest sense as motivated and contextualized. With the full truth of human actions made narratively available, the ambition of Tutu's even-handedness is to make it possible for the people of South Africa to express forgiveness without forgetting what is just and what is unjust. As Tutu continues in his foreword, "I do not for a single moment question the sincerity of those who believed that they were defending their country and what they understood to be its Western Christian values against the atheistic Communist onslaught. No, I do not call their motives into question. I do, however, condemn the policy they applied" (1: 14). In general even-handedness asks for a personal accounting of one's actions. To account for oneself even-handedly is to find the words to explain oneself without either making excuses or denying the injustice of one's actions. Even-handedness also asks for a given kind of response to a person's account of the truth, an attending to and accepting of the account as it is given, an attending that at the same time holds firm to a view of the injustice of a system such as apartheid. Expressing and attending to a personal, narrative truth with an understanding of what is systemically just and unjust is—as Tutu explains—the way to reconciliation, and reconciliation is the way out of a racist past into a democratic future. At least that is Tutu's ambition for his rhetoric of even-handedness.

Yet, as the experience of transition from apartheid to democracy revealed, narrative tensions between forgiveness and justice, between personal motivation and political doctrine, constantly threatened to tear the people of South Africa apart. Near the end of his foreword to the TRC report, Tutu acknowledges the tension, directly linking the narrative specificity of human truth with the psychological demands of personal and political reconciliation:

> We should accept that truth has emerged even though it has initially alienated people from one another. The truth can be, and often is, divisive. However, it is only on the basis of truth that true reconciliation can take

place. True reconciliation is not easy; it is not cheap. . . . I want to make a heartfelt plea to my white fellow South Africans. On the whole we have been exhilarated by the magnanimity of those who should by rights be consumed by bitterness and a lust for revenge; who instead have time after time shown an astonishing magnanimity and willingness to forgive. . . . I have been sad-dened by what has appeared to be a mean-spiritedness in some of the lead-ership in the white community. They should be saying: "How fortunate we are that these people do not want to treat us as we treated them." (1: 18)

Even-handed reconciliation is not easy because it is threatened at every turn by human emotions such as bitterness, lust for revenge, mean-spiritedness, emotions which breed distrust, emotions acquired through the divisive years of apartheid rule. Reconciliation can only take place when the divisive emo-tions of bitterness and mean-spiritedness are given up in favor of emotions such as magnanimity, a willingness to forgive, gratitude. These are the emotions of even-handedness, emotions which are far from neutral, emotions which open people to each other.

Even-handedly listening to the testimony given at TRC hearings by victims as well as perpetrators of human rights abuses asks for an attending to the sin-cerity of others in their giving an account of themselves, listening to their stories of torture, rape, and murder without giving in to bitterness, mean-spiritedness, or the thirst for some kind of retribution. For Tutu even-handedly accepting people's narrative accounts of their motives is an openness to truth as others experience and express it, whatever that truth is, however it is told. It is an atti-tude of openness to others through an openness to their choice of words. More importantly though, an attitude of openness to the motives of others is meant to invite and encourage in those perpetrators of human rights abuses who gave account of their actions a re-evaluation of the words they choose when they decide to express what they did. Theirs is the obligation to speak in ways that make clear to others what they did, why they did it, and how they feel about it. The point, then, is not to speak in ways that justify. The point is to find ways to speak that ask from others an acceptance of intentions, motives, and per-spectives. The reconciliation that is meant to follow from Tutu's proposal for even-handed acts of speaking and listening is not a thin tolerance for individual perspectives on shared events. It is less a matter of a community contenting itself with conflicting, even contradictory justifications for who did what when and why. It is more a matter of encouraging individuals to make themselves available for persuasive participation in a human community they are, through their words, creating together.

My general characterization of Tutu's rhetoric of even-handedness already seems to overreach common perceptions of equanimity. Magnanimity and a willingness to forgive—the stuff of reconciliation—seem to ask a lot of South Africans, whose lives were poisoned by apartheid. It certainly asks more than is asked from a kind of dispassionate justice which seeks the truth of human actions without emotion—something which would seem more akin to a principled commitment to not compromise on what is just and right and true. Tutu's rhetoric of compassionate compromise—his desire for framing commitments to justice in terms of expressions of forgiveness—seems to ask far more than anyone might possibly be willing or able to accept.

Not everyone did share Tutu's view of reconciliation as compassionate compromise. His was not even the view of even-handedness advocated for by the TRC as a whole. Rather, an uncompromising, dispassionate understanding of even-handedness in the expressing and experiencing of people's accounts of themselves seems closer to the view of the TRC as a whole. In the final report of the TRC, even-handedness is described by the committee as a whole as a third perspective for understanding apartheid, the struggle against apartheid, and the human rights abuses committed by both sides: "While each side may put forward reasonable and quite understandable explanations or justifications for such actions, the task of the third perspective, that of the Commission, is to recognise that these accounts are not equivalent. This non-equivalence means that protagonists in the thirty-year conflict were motivated by quite different political perspectives" (vol. 5: 276). The appeal to motive in this definition of even-handedness resonates with Tutu's use of the term, although it is clear from the description of the commission's third perspective that the motives of apartheid's supporters are different from the motives of those who struggled against apartheid. Motives do not make wrong actions right, but they do ground actions more or less securely in principles of right and wrong. The third perspective of the TRC accepts neither the legitimacy of apartheid nor the legitimacy of human rights abuses committed by either side during the struggle. This perspective takes a point of view from outside history to provide a rhetorical structure which places limits on personal narratives of human action, discursively constraining both the legitimacy of acts committed in the name of a racist state as well as the legitimacy of acts committed in the name of dismantling a racist state. A third perspective is one through which the past is described as independently as possible of the views and values of those who participated in the apartheid government and those who actively fought against it. It is in this way an attempt to step back from the flow of South Africa's recent history, an attempt at a kind of neutrality, a perspective less concerned with defining a future and more concerned with describing a past. Here consideration of motives is less conciliatory, decidedly more focused on impartiality and the search for truth than on magnanimity and the desire for reconciliation.

The impartiality of a more neutral third perspective and the magnanimity of forgiveness are not necessarily incompatible, although they are difficult to narratively weave together. The dispositions of impartiality and magnanimity are in fundamental tension in the rhetoric of the TRC. The success—or, as some have described it, the failure—of the TRC is the extent to which it could turn the impartiality of an even-handed third perspective on the past into the foundation for an even-handed magnanimity of reconciliation. At stake in evaluations of the success or failure of the TRC are matters of emotional satisfaction. These are issues of how fully the rhetoric of the TRC allows for expressing the concerns South Africans carry from their past into their future.

While I appreciate the careful choice of the term "even-handed" used by the TRC in characterizing its approach to testimony, I also find the characterization to lack the kind of explanatory potential needed to fully describe the emotional challenges posed to South Africans by ambition for both impartiality and magnanimity. The term "even-handed" hardly seems to capture the disposition required of those who participated in the hearings, especially the commissioners of the TRC whose role was to sit through days upon days of testimonies of human rights abuses. The intensity of the experience of daily hearing horrific testimony is described by Wendy Orr in her memoir recounting her time as a TRC commissioner, from the frustration of feeling that she had wasted three years of her life (231), to the unspeakable sorrow of hearing the confession of a young conscript who became for her "every young white man who had fought a faceless enemy for no reason other than that he was ordered to do so. I wept, as I had done so many times in my TRC work, but this time I wept for myself and the little brother I had lost forever" (259). Antjie Krog gives a similar account in *Country of My Skull*, her book documenting her experiences as a reporter covering the TRC. She describes how reporters who followed the TRC suffered from the strain of day after day hearing accounts of human rights abuses. Many became ill and felt themselves alienated from families and friends. None found it possible to adopt a third perspective and step outside the experience of listening to the tragedies of their country's past. The memoirs of Orr and Krog remind us that more was required of the participants in and observers of the TRC than even-handed impartiality. Those who participated in and followed the TRC were emotionally engaged in the events. They were looking for something —whether forgiveness or justice or simply the truth—at the same time they were asked for a kind of magnanimity in the face of what they at times experienced as far more painful than productive.

Yet commissioners like Orr and reporters like Krog did risk the pain of participating in the TRC because doing so held out the promise of a sense of connectedness that could restore in South Africans a hope for their lives together. It was the pain and the joy, as Krog put it, of participating in "the birth of this country's language itself" (42) or, in Pumla Gobodo-Madikizela's words, of learning "a vocabulary of compromise and tolerance," a way of talking and listening in which citizens settle "differences through the politics of contestation and compromise among equals," a process of dialogue that "seeks to create new relationships and repair old ones" (126).

Creating and repairing relationships through dialogue sounds like negotiation, and negotiation sounds, much like even-handedness, like an inadequate characterization of what it took to participate in the TRC. Negotiating disagreements, settling differences through the politics of contest and compromise, is a noble ambition, but putting it this way also minimizes the emotional strain that makes it so difficult to create and repair relationships through dialogue. Without a fuller characterization of the emotional richness of rhetorics of reconciliation we get only a distorted sense of what it takes and what must be done to create new relationships and repair old ones. To get a sense of the personal demands of this rhetorical ambition, to get a sense of how those personal demands relate to political ideals, and to get a sense of the extent to which the discourse of the TRC evolved to satisfy those demands, involves returning to the origins of the TRC in the negotiations between the Afrikaner government and the ANC, negotiations which secured enough stability to make the transition from apartheid to democracy.

Key to the success of the negotiated settlement in South Africa was an agreement on the Afrikaner demand for amnesty. A provision for amnesty was the last-minute compromise that cinched the negotiated settlement for a transitional government. Even these high-level political negotiations were strained by the growing violence, which only heightened the mistrust and animosity among the parties. Both sides recognized that a provision for amnesty was necessary to establish enough trust in a post-apartheid future for people on both sides of the conflict to feel they could put down their weapons. Before agreeing to let go their hold on the government, the National Party demanded guarantees that individuals would be granted amnesty from prosecution for acts committed during apartheid rule. They feared a victor's justice, and what they wanted was a blanket amnesty. What they got was a provision for deciding amnesties on a case-by-case basis. Both sides agreed that amnesty would be granted as part of a process of uncovering as completely as possible the truth of who did what during apartheid. Forgiveness in the form of amnesty was tied to accountability for the injustices of apartheid.

As crucial as it was for achieving a peaceful transition to democracy, compromise over questions of amnesty for crimes committed during apartheid left both sides in the negotiations feeling less than satisfied. F. W. de Klerk, the last apartheid president of South Africa, bluntly put the dissatisfaction of the National Party over the establishment of the TRC and the question of amnesty as "probably our greatest failure during the negotiating process" (289). But the prospect of not finding a compromise promised to be far more unsatisfying. The threat of a prolonged civil war, continued international isolation, and the very real prospect of South Africa's economic collapse compelled both parties to the negotiations to find some way to mediate their differences. Compromise on the issue of amnesty opened the way for the 1993 interim Constitution of South Africa, which contains the amnesty clause in its postamble:

> The adoption of this Constitution lays the secure foundation for the people of South Africa to transcend the divisions and strife of the past, which generated gross violations of human rights, the transgression of humanitarian principles in violent conflicts and a legacy of hatred, fear, guilt and revenge.
>
> These can now be addressed on the basis that there is a need for understanding but not for vengeance, a need for reparation but not for retaliation, a need for ubuntu but not for victimisation.
>
> In order to advance such reconciliation and reconstruction, amnesty shall be granted in respect of acts, omissions and offences associated with political objectives and committed in the course of the conflicts of the past. To this end, Parliament under this Constitution shall adopt a law determining a firm cut-off date, which shall be a date after 8 October 1990 and before 6 December 1993, and providing for the mechanisms, criteria and procedures, including tribunals, if any, through which such amnesty shall be dealt with at any time after the law has been passed.
>
> With this Constitution and these commitments we, the people of South Africa, open a new chapter in the history of our country.

This passage directs the South African Parliament to legislate a commission for deciding amnesty cases. The resulting legislation, the 1995 National Unity and Reconciliation Act, established the TRC, repeating these words from the postamble, "there is a need for understanding but not for vengeance, a need for reparation but not for retaliation, a need for ubuntu but not for victimization." In both documents decisions about amnesty are joined to assurances against vengeance, retaliation, and victimization as well as ambitions for understanding, reparations, and *ubuntu*. For the purpose of describing Tutu's balancing of forgiveness and justice as an elaboration of the interim constitution's mandate, note that the word *ubuntu* is included in both the constitutional postamble and the National Unity and Recovery Act. The use of the word creates a rhetorical opening. *Ubuntu* seems to not be parallel with the other words—"understanding" and "reparations"—with which it is paired. The dissonance of *ubuntu* is in fact crucial to the expression of what it means to join a commitment to truth and justice with an equal commitment to forgiveness and reconciliation.

The final report of the TRC references the interim constitution to argue that the commission's mission was to nurture through appeal to *ubuntu* a caring ethos out of growing anger and insecurity, to "build on the humanitarian and caring ethos of the South African Constitution . . . despite growing anger and insecurity in the midst of high levels of crime in South Africa" (vol. 1: 127). This interpretation of the TRC's constitutional mandate shifts emphasis from amnesty claims of perpetrators to the dignity of victims as well as perpetrators. The report describes the TRC mandate as one of promoting "respect for human life and dignity and for a revival of ubuntu; a commitment that included the strengthening of the restorative dimensions of justice" (vol. 1: 126). Here the political dimension of legal justice, the initial concern for amnesty which mandated formation of the TRC, is augmented through appeal to the "sources of communal healing and restoration" in Judeo-Christian and African traditional values, where "the fundamental importance of ubuntu must be highlighted" (vol. 1: 127). Through appeal to *ubuntu,* amnesty becomes more than a legal reprieve or a forgiving of past transgressions; it becomes an occasion for reintegration. It would be the height of cynicism to read these claims as nothing more than political maneuverings or institutional justifications, for it is here that appeals to *ubuntu* provide a vocabulary for reconciliation.

In and around the rhetoric of the TRC, the word *ubuntu* also more fully articulates the emotional experience of finding an even-handed third perspective. Whether and how uses of the word invoke, assign, and transform understandings of and expectations for even-handedness among victims and perpetrators and TRC commissioners are issues explicitly raised by Susan van der Merwe's appeal to *ubuntu* in her testimony before the TRC.

Susan van der Merwe last saw her husband on November 1, 1978. They had just finished breakfast at their home in Swartklip, in the Thabazimbi region of

South Africa, just south of the border with Botswana. She left for her job as a teacher. He drove to his mother's farm approximately sixty kilometers away. As she was to learn later, her husband—an Afrikaner farmer—had stopped to give a ride to four men, later identified as members of Umkhonto we Sizwe, the guerilla faction of the ANC, who had crossed into the area from Botswana to contact farmers and identify possible bases of operation for their war against the apartheid government. The guerilla fighters abducted van der Merwe, shot him, and left him in the bush for dead. His body was never found.

On September 23, 1996, after the transition in South Africa from apartheid to democracy, Susan van der Merwe made a public appeal before the TRC: "The Tswanas have an idiom which I learned from my husband which goes 'a person is a person by other people, a person is only a person with other people.' We do have this duty to each other. The survival of our people in this country depends on our co-operation with each other. My plea to you is, help people throw their weapons away. . . . No person's life is a waste. Every person's life is too precious" (vol. 1: 127–28). The Tswana idiom to which van der Merwe appeals in support of her plea for cooperation and peace is familiar enough in contemporary South Africa: "umuntu ngumuntu ngabantu," or "a person is a person through other people," or simply *ubuntu.*

Van der Merwe's appeal to *ubuntu* figures centrally in the narrative of the TRC's final report, published in 1998, in which the commissioners explicitly appeal to *ubuntu* to explain their understanding of their constitutional mandate to restore "the human and civil dignity of victims" (vol. 1: 125). A commitment to human dignity was for the commissioners a commitment to restorative justice, an ambition which "challenges South Africans to build on the humanitarian and caring ethos of the South African Constitution and to emphasize the need for reparation rather than retaliation" (vol. 1: 127). In the report, justification for emphasis on restorative justice and a need for reparation is supported negatively at first, with a quote from an opinion written by Justice Langa of the South African Constitutional Court in the first death-penalty case heard by the court after the transition to democracy. In his opinion declaring the death penalty unconstitutional, Justice Langa wrote, "During violent conflicts and times when violent crime is rife, distraught members of society decry the loss of *ubuntu.* Thus, heinous crimes are the antithesis of ubuntu. Treatment that is cruel, inhuman or degrading is bereft of ubuntu" (vol. 1: 127). The death penalty, because it is punitive and not restorative, is cruel, inhuman, degrading, a punishment that only perpetuates a society's loss of human values. Having disparaged retributive justice as bereft of *ubuntu,* the final report of the TRC next argues in support of the claim for restorative justice by referencing the work of the commission itself, work from which "a spontaneous call has arisen among sections of the population for a return to ubuntu." Evidence of the spontaneous call is provided through quotation of Susan van der Merwe's plea (vol. 1: 127). The argument for restorative justice through appeal to *ubuntu* seems decidedly circular. Susan van der Merwe's plea hardly seems spontaneous as it was made before a commission which was itself legislated through a constitutional appeal to *ubuntu*. And while the interim Constitution of South Africa may appear to ground appeals to *ubuntu*, use of the term in the postamble suggests what Justice Langa's reference to the term in the Constitutional Court makes clear: *ubuntu* has a meaning and a value that are read into rather than arising out of the documents themselves.

Erik Doxtader makes a similar point in *With Faith in the Works of Words*, arguing that elision of *understanding, ubuntu,* and *amnesty* in the text of the interim constitution confuses more than it clarifies, leaving it to the TRC itself to define in practice the meanings of these terms. Referencing TRC Chairman Desmond Tutu's response to the question of ambiguities in uses of *ubuntu*, Doxtader notes that the term "defies strict analysis precisely because the idea of ubuntu holds and performs a movement in which identity takes form in a manner that," quoting Tutu, "is not isolated from others, because that way is death" (71). Because of the ambiguity in the word's uses, Doxtader argues that we can best make sense of the South African transition to democracy by focusing less on the meaning and use of such fluid terms as *ubuntu* and *amnesty* and more on *reconciliation,* a word he finds more open to a productive rhetorical analysis because deliberation about reconciliation can be understood as both a means to the end of apartheid and as an end in itself. As Doxtader describes it, deliberations about the meaning of reconciliation among different people, at different times, and for different purposes generated discursive spaces in which "each party renounced (at least temporarily) their historical 'duty,' demonstrated a willingness to talk and to listen in good faith, and accepted that there was a difference between violence and heated disagreement about how to define the form and content of transition" (289).

Without contesting this claim, I want to make the case that the meanings of *ubuntu* created through the TRC hearings did more than obfuscate. As seen in the emotionally demanding experience of listening to the testimony of apartheid's perpetrators and its victims, even-handedness, negotiations, third perspectives are all, like heated disagreement, thin characterizations of the vulnerability that was required for the people of South Africa to discover in acts of giving and hearing public testimony what it means to experience being human through the experience of the humanity of others.

The TRC commissioners in particular needed to be more than disinterestedly even-handed if they were to become participants in the building of a democratic country. They had to listen to the stories of loss and pain, to hear the whole horrible truth without becoming embittered and unforgiving. As models of democratic participation for citizens to emulate, they had to demonstrate what it is to be even-handed—impartial and magnanimous, forgiving as well as just. They had to show how it is possible for people to make themselves vulnerable to each other in ways that do not sacrifice the integrity that their sovereignty requires.

As chairman of the TRC, Tutu with his conciliatory gesture of even-handedness motioned the people of South Africa toward the path of facing who they are and affirming what they might become, describing the imperative to remember less as a hope for the future and more as an obligation to the past: "To accept national amnesia would . . . in effect be to victimize the victims of apartheid a second time around. We would have denied something that contributed to the identity of who we were" (29). The people of South Africa should not deny the tragic past that has made them who they are, for such a denial would only perpetuate the tragedy. They also should not allow the tragedy to completely define who they are or who they may become. As Tutu wrote, "To forgive is not just to be altruistic. It is the best form of self-interest. What dehumanizes you inexorably dehumanizes me. It gives people resilience, enabling them to survive and emerge still human despite all efforts to dehumanize them" (*Truth and Reconciliation Commission of South Africa Report*, 1: 31). Tutu's even-handedness refuses to dehumanize the victims of apartheid by refusing to compromise on what is just and unjust, while also refusing to constrain the humanity of post-apartheid South Africans of all colors by holding out hope for forgiveness. Letting go and potentially forgetting injury and loss only contributes to degradation, victimizing the victims by denying their suffering, the sacrifices they made, and the benefits others have gained through their sacrifices and suffering. Forgetting and so forgiving too easily is as degrading as deciding that not forgetting means not forgiving. The blanket refusal to express forgiveness distorts the suffering and sacrifices of the victims of apartheid, denying them their due resilience. Here the rhetorical challenge of even-handedness is also its greatest benefit, keeping integrated the people and purposes that provide our lives with meaning, however tragic or bittersweet. For Tutu, *ubuntu* is the strongest expression of this sense of integrating past, present, and future: "Our people must show the world God has given us a great gift, *ubuntu*. . . . However, the world should also know that forgiveness and reconciliation are not cheap. . . . *Ubuntu* says I am human only because you are human. If I undermine your humanity, I dehumanize myself. You must do what you can to maintain this great harmony, which is perpetually undermined by resentment, anger, desire for vengeance. That's why African jurisprudence is restorative rather than retributive" (quoted in English, 645).

In the discourse of the TRC, *ubuntu* is a term that did more than describe the nature of personhood; it became a rationale for encouraging South Africans to rediscover their personhood through the process of national reconciliation. Tutu made it clear that reconciliation comes at a cost, and for some the cost seemed too high.

Dialogues of empathy and forgiveness through which people can reclaim their humanity are difficult not only because they are emotionally draining. Those dialogues also challenge the human capacity for expressing meaningfully that which defies meaning. Being even-handed in the strong sense suggested by Tutu—comprehending another's expression of his or her human experience, recognizing in it that there is right and wrong, that there is suffering and hope, finding in that comprehension and recognition the possibility of reconciliation —demands of people that they are open and honest to each other, that they become vulnerable and have integrity. It demands commitment and engagement and reflection. It is the rhetorical challenge of saying what one needs and wants to say to others who have every reason to distrust or even disregard what they hear. Because there is such antipathy, the other side of the rhetorical challenge is to also make every effort to attend to what the other is trying to say. To be even-handed is to speak and listen to one another while remaining aware of the attitudes and feelings people cultivate to protect themselves from each other. The demands of this kind of even-handedness are exemplified by TRC member Pumla Gobodo-Madikizela's gesture of sympathy toward one of the most notorious apartheid government agents, Eugene de Kock.

De Kock was former commanding officer of apartheid death squads. His unit, the African Police Counterinsurgency Unit, was based on a farm, Vlakplaas, located west of Pretoria, the administrative capital of South Africa. De Kock and the other officers of Vlakplaas were responsible for executions of suspected apartheid opponents, such as the February 1989 ambush and murder of three student activists—Portia Shabangu, Thabo Mohale, and Derrick Mashobane— near Bhunya, Swaziland (*Truth and Reconciliation Commission of South Africa Report* 2: 133), or the planting of a car bomb which killed three black policemen, including Amos Themba Faku and Mbambalala Glen Mgoduka. The latter incident, which became known as the Motherwell bombing, was the subject of de Kock's first appearance before the TRC. In exchange for his testimony regarding the bombing, as well as other kidnappings and murders undertaken by

Vlakplaas forces, de Kock applied to the TRC for amnesty. While he did not receive amnesty for the abuses he took part in, his cooperation was crucial for the establishment of the truth. In the summation of its efforts to use the appeal of amnesty to coax the truth of apartheid from its functionaries, the final report of the TRC acknowledges, "it was largely [de Kock] who broke the code of silence," and so, the "ironic truth is that what brought them to the Commission was the fullness of disclosure made by an individual often painted as the arch-villain of the apartheid era" (vol. 5: 202). It is no exaggeration to characterize de Kock as the arch-villain of apartheid. He was even given the nickname "Prime Evil" in the press during its coverage of the TRC.

Because he was such a prominent participant in the TRC hearings, the commission also concluded that the media attention he drew distorted focus on the responsibility for apartheid shared by ordinary citizens of South Africa. The commission admits to participating in this distortion. The issue was a choice between "thoughtless submission rather than thoughtful accountability," in order to ensure "the future is different from the past" (vol. 1: 132). The commission admits to failing in the task of providing political accountability and moral responsibility for two reasons. First, the focus on high-profile cases such as de Kock's, a focus which has drawn attention away from everyday human-rights violations, allowed ordinary South Africans to not see themselves as perpetrators. For the commission, "only by recognising the potential for evil in each one of us that we can take full responsibility for ensuring that such evil will never be repeated" (vol. 1: 133). Second, the failure, according to the commission, was to not "grasp the significance of individual victims' testimony before the Commission." To grasp the significance of those stories is for the nation to "use these stories to sharpen its moral conscience and to ensure that, never again, will it gradually atrophy to the point where personal responsibility is abdicated" (133). Further, to grasp the meaning of the stories and take responsibility means "that a great deal of attention must be given to an altered sense of responsibility; namely the duty or obligation of those who have benefitted so much (through racially privileged education, unfair access to land, business opportunities and so on) to contribute to the present and future reconstruction of our society" (134).

Grasping the meaning of the stories told before the TRC, getting a grip on their personal impacts, requires an empathy from ordinary citizens, an availability to others that can strain ambitions for even-handedness. As important as it no doubt was for South Africans to watch and listen to the TRC hearings, observing could not by itself transform someone like de Kock from the personification of apartheid into a person responsible for his actions. Still, despite the nationwide media distraction that his appearance may have provided, it also functioned on a personal level for him and for at least a few of his victims. After his first appearance before the TRC, during which he testified about his involvement in the Motherwell bombing, de Kock requested a private meeting with the widows of the black police officers his car bomb had killed. The widows of Amos Themba Faku and Mbambalala Glen Mgoduka agreed to meet with him. In her role on the TRC as a human rights commissioner, Gobodo-Madikizela debriefed the widows, Pearl Faku and Doreen Mgoduka. They related that they had been moved to tears by their meeting with the murderer of their husbands because de Kock had persuaded them he recognized the depth of their pain. As Faku related to Gobodo-Madikizela, "I could hear him, but I was overwhelmed by emotion, and I was just nodding, as a way of saying yes, I forgive you. I hope that when he sees our tears, he knows that they are not only tears for our husbands, but tears for him as well. . . . I would like to hold him by the hand, and show him that there is a future, and that he can still change" (14–15). The widows—Pearl Faku and Doreen Mgoduka—listened to de Kock with a kind of magnanimity and willingness to forgive that would seem on the surface to belie their grief. Yet their compassion for de Kock, expressed in the tears they shed for him as well as for their husbands, must be understood less as a denial of their grief and more as a refusal of bitterness.

No one could compel such victims as Pearl Faku and Doreen Mgoduka to forgive those who committed human rights abuses against them. There were those who found themselves unable to forgive. But as Gobodo-Madikizela points out, victims who are incapable of forgiveness, who hang on to feelings of resentment, may not know what else to do. The emotions of anger and desire for vengeance can become "a symbol of the perpetrator's powerful grip over the victim, they are a burden that hangs over the victim and at once creates a dependency on the hateful emotions and denies the victim a chance to come to terms with what happened" (96). For Gobodo-Madikizela the act of forgiving is an opportunity for openness to others, a kind of reversal of the vulnerability the victim experienced at the hands of the victimizer. It can enact what she terms a "paradox of remorse" in which a victim empathizes with the pain of regret felt by the perpetrator (100). As painful and confusing as such a process no doubt is, it can lead to dialogue that is both "punishment and rehabilitation" for the victimizer (120). In addition to humbling and humanizing the perpetrator, dialogue allows the victim to feel more human as well, by providing a "process of reclaiming self-efficacy," in which "reciprocating with empathy and forgiveness in the face of the perpetrator's remorse restores to many victims the sense that they are once again capable of effecting a profound difference in the moral community" (128). We can only imagine that this is the kind of empathy Pearl Faku had in mind when she expresses her hope that de Kock could still change.

Curious about the exchange between Faku and de Kock, Gobodo-Madikizela asked de Kock about his meeting with the widows of the Motherwell bombing. In a trembling voice he explained the depth of his distress upon meeting with the women: "I wish I could do much more than [say] I'm sorry. I wish there was a way of bringing their bodies back alive. I wish I could say, 'Here are your husbands' . . . but unfortunately . . . I have to live with it" (32). Understanding that she is listening to a person who is making himself emotionally vulnerable, she is moved, and in her response to his words and his demeanor, "Relating to him in the only way one does in such human circumstances," Gobodo-Madikizela explains, "I touched his shaking hand, surprising myself. But it was clenched, cold, and rigid, as if he were holding something back, as if he were holding on to some withering but still vital form of his old self" (32). Recognizing her empathy for another human being, Gobodo-Madikizela is also confused about her response to someone who has demonstrated a capacity for terrible evil. She struggles with knowing that he has killed repeatedly over the years. She struggles with the suspicion that he is responsible for the deaths of people close to her. She struggles with feeling he was holding back, that in opening herself to his agony she has betrayed something of herself to a murderer and a liar.

Expressions of vulnerability such as Gobodo-Madikizela's do surprise. We cannot in every instance safeguard our availability to the presence of others, and when we cannot we are bewildered by our responses. In the presence of de Kock especially, knowledge of his ruthlessness would justify heightened vigilance. Seeing de Kock as "Prime Evil" means keeping him at a distance. Such vigilance can be motivated by, at the same time it is a means of suppressing, the anger and fear, the horror and confusion, all the emotions that would be aroused in the presence of someone who is so threatening. The challenge Gobodo-Madikizela takes up by deciding to engage with de Kock as a person with feelings rather than as an agent of apartheid is the challenge of accepting the shock of finding herself completely vulnerable. She takes up the challenge of experiencing herself as torn, at a loss. It is the experience of having the narrative integrity of one's life unravel.

Later in Cape Town, during a break in his appearance before the TRC, de Kock asks to meet briefly with Gobodo-Madikizela. As she recounts, "With an intent look on his face, he thanked me 'for the other day,' a reference to our meeting in the prison interview room. Then, with an expression that seemed to reflect genuine amazement, he said, 'You know Pumla, that was my trigger hand you touched'" (39). Gobodo-Madikizela recounts the impact of his words, "I have not, up until now, been able to free myself from the grip of that statement nor to soften its visceral impact" (39). That impact expressed itself the next day when, lying awake in bed, she could not lift the arm with which she had touched him, "I couldn't feel with it, as if my body were rejecting a foreign organ illegitimately planted" (41).

She relates that the gesture had its impact on de Kock as well, that "he too was struggling with what being touched meant." She continues by speculating that "It seemed to have evoked a trail of thought that brought him not so much to what it meant to be touched but to what it meant to be touched *there*, on *that* hand. Whether or not this was the first thing that came to mind for him, his way of communicating his anxiety about my gesture was to 'split off' the hand from the rest of his body, to excise the part that did the killing, as if the 'trigger hand' had gone off on a killing rampage by itself" (41).

Gobodo-Madikizela struggled for days to make sense of her gesture of compassion, concluding finally, "My act of empathy had drawn me into intimate complicity with him. This too is possible. . . . If evil is humanity turned against itself, then conflict and contradiction are fundamental to its nature. And if evil is in essence self-contradictory, then the interpretive conflicts engendered by his statement—the turmoil that seemed to burst from its surface—merely point to the urgency of de Kock's inner wrestling and the psychological instability inherent in the state of mind we call evil" (46–47). These are not for Gobodo-Madikizela abstract concerns; they are matters of being and becoming human, matters of *ubuntu*. As she puts it, "Philosophical questions can and should give way and be subsumed to *human* questions, for in the end we are a society of people and not of ideas, a fragile web of interdependent humans, not of stances" (125).

In *Country of My Skull*, Krog describes human relations not easily reconciled, struggling with what it is to live in the fragile web of human interactions. Krog recounts a discussion with a white farmer from the Free State who remarked on the TRC: "if these things were done to me, I would hate deeply and passionately. . . . the fact that they didn't just shows you that blacks are not even able to *hate* sufficiently" (213). Krog then quotes the response of clinical psychologist Nomfundo Walaza:

> I think the Soweto uprisings were proof enough what blacks can do when they are being pushed too far. But what we're probably dealing with here is people who are coming from a culture with a capitalist notion of existence in the world, where you have things for yourself and your group, the people that look like you. And the other notion that people can actually

share things is totally incomprehensible to them. When whites came to the country . . . it seemed that black people initially were happy to share things and to give over . . . but that kind of sharing went wrong. This whole concept of ubuntu that is being bandied about all over the place, that went horribly wrong. (213)

Not only did *ubuntu* go horribly wrong in the way it left Africans open to the exploitations of apartheid, Walaza thinks it goes wrong as a rhetorical value urging performances of forgiveness during the TRC hearings as well. *Ubuntu* cannot easily bridge the cultural divide because if it could it would betray the pain and suffering shared by de Kock, Faku, Gobodo-Madikizela, Mgoduka, van der Merwe, and the countless others whose lives were destroyed by apartheid. I do not take Walaza's point to be that *ubuntu* is trivial, just that it can be made too convenient. Appeal to *ubuntu* rather than leading people into relationships where they share their range of emotions with each other can also and at the same time be used to allow people an easy out that provides them the comfort of limited conflict and avoids bridging the cultural divide separating European from African.

It is in this sense that the apparent success of the TRC made *ubuntu* available as a convenient symbol. As a symbol *ubuntu* could become commodified, and commodification, far from promoting or precluding an understanding of *ubuntu*, offers little comfort and creates much confusion. If a return to dignity can be neither directly experienced nor straightforwardly expressed, what sense might it make to consider the prospect of restoring relations of dignity through the production and interpretation of texts? It is not simply empty hope that drives talk of restoring relationships of dignity through uses of documents such as the South African Constitution. At the same time, cynicism about political compromise curtails the prospects of there being any progress. Perhaps the degree to which the documents do not satisfy is the degree to which the indigenous concept of *ubuntu* fails to become fully realized. Perhaps the extent to which hope can be kept open, and *ubuntu* can function, is the extent to which the tension between reality and rhetoric becomes available for manipulation.

Tutu called for South Africans to face who they are and affirm who they might become, in words describing the imperative to remember less as a hope for the future and more as an obligation to the past: "To accept national amnesia would . . . in effect be to victimize the victims of apartheid a second time around. We would have denied something that contributed to the identity of who we were" (*No Future*, 29). Loss of memory would set people free from history, uncoupling who they are from what they might become. The loss of memory, the loss of words to recall the pain of the past, would only contribute to further degradation, victimizing the victims by denying the sacrifices they made and the benefits others have gained.

Forgiving as forgetting is the worst form of ahistorical decontextualization. To misconstrue forgiveness with a desire to leave the past behind only mischaracterizes dehumanization as an aberration and so forgets the formative power of experiences and perceptions of injury. A language allowing forgiveness as forgetting mischaracterizes the injury of dehumanization by distancing the present from the past. In his use of *ubuntu,* Tutu calls for a rhetoric of connectedness that is not ahistorical and that does not distance past from present. His is a way of preserving humanity by narrating collective accountability for both recollection of who we are and affirmation of who we might become.

The rhetorical challenge of *ubuntu,* the challenge of admitting wounds of the past without allowing pain to embitter the present, is also *ubuntu*'s greatest benefit, keeping integrated across time and place the people and purposes that provide meaning. Among other things, *ubuntu* provides a rhetorical strategy for restraining the desire for retribution that only perpetuates cycles of divisiveness. It reminds us that the fabric of society is woven by rhetorical agents and audiences bound to each other in their making of meaning.

As with so much else in the creating of democracy in South Africa, the TRC provided a collective narrative of nation-building. As with any national narrative the experiences and participation of all citizens are vital for success and are also always uneven at best. The ambition of providing people a narrative of national sovereignty misappropriates and misconstrues their experiences of vulnerability. People's ambitions and experiences are far less unified and their vulnerability far greater. Reconciling with the past requires far more vulnerability than conciliation. It is far more fragile because it is open to otherness. There is the difficulty of reconciling, the pain of it, the courage of it.

Issues of even-handedness, issues of balancing forgiveness and justice, issues of *ubuntu,* reemerged in January 2010 when South African President Jacob Zuma was reported to be considering a presidential pardon for de Kock. Gobodo-Madikizela argued in an editorial for serious consideration for de Kock's pardon. In this she opposed those like Christi van der Westhuizen who argued against the pardon. For van der Westhuizen, de Kock is simply unpardonable. Van der Westhuizen's claim is grounded in de Kock's efforts to ban a quote from her book, *White Power & the Rise and Fall of the National Party,* in which a former apartheid official refers skeptically to the claim that de Kock and others were "braising meat and drinking for hours next to a corpse they had set on fire" (311). De Kock's failed legal challenge only demonstrates for van der Westhuizen the guilt of de Kock and the pathology of apartheid. It is "white power at work," she writes in an editorial against the pardon, "a white man who committed multiple murders in the name of white supremacy launching court applications from jail to block books about the very system for which he mercilessly killed." What troubles van der Westhuizen most about the challenge is its confrontation of her book, which she regards as "a personal and political attempt by another Afrikaner to confront the horrors of apartheid for which white people are culpable but in which De Kock played a particularly pernicious role."

The issue of culpability is precisely the point for Gobodo-Madikizela in her cautious consideration of de Kock's application for presidential pardon. For Gobodo-Madikizela public outcry over de Kock's possible pardon recalls "predictable images of 'the evil one' ingrained in our collective memory and of the deeds committed by the man who has to carry the burden of uncomfortable truths about our past." This is not to say that de Kock does not carry the burden of guilt for the crimes he committed. Instead her point is that de Kock is made to carry responsibility for others who then do not need to feel themselves responsible for either the past or the future. Meaningful reconciliation requires "acknowledgement of past wrongs by perpetrators, bystanders and beneficiaries alike." When every citizen of South Africa refuses the opposed rhetorics of vilification and victimization, then Mandela's promise of "never again" can be a reality. The rhetoric of reconciliation can be a reality, as Gobodo-Madikizela concludes, "in our country if we face the fact that 'Prime Evil' is not only on de Kock's face, but has the potential to be written on yours and mine, too."

Chapter 7

TSOTSI, DISTRICT 9, AND THE VISUALIZATION OF VULNERABLE RHETORICS

The ambition for even-handedness formalized in the South African Truth and Reconciliation Commission—an ambition that the people of South Africa admit to each other the injustices of the past while encouraging among themselves productive dialogue in the present—could well remain nothing more than an ambition if it is not taken up more informally in venues other than the public hearings of the TRC. As a number of critics of the TRC have commented, the formal processes of amnesty application, legal challenge, and testifying removed the demands for accountability from ordinary citizens to concentrate them in public figures such as Eugene de Kock, "Prime Evil," whose amnesty application to the TRC drew considerable media attention. I believe the criticism justified as far as it goes. Certainly the requirements for a rhetoric of citizen participation in the collective articulation of a common good include accepting vulnerabilities to limited and unequally distributed material resources intertwined with vulnerabilities to limited and unevenly focused attitudinal resources.

Given limits on material and attitudinal resources, citizens who participate in the discourse of a democracy must face the challenge of finding ways of expressing a common good that do not misconstrue authority, responsibility, or sovereignty. Pumla Gobodo-Madikizela's response to the possibility of de Kock's presidential pardon faces this challenge because it is an argument for perceiving the pardon not strictly in terms of the expressions of outrage at the possibility that someone so guilty could be freed to live among the innocent, but as an opportunity for putting into words what it means for all citizens of South Africa to risk taking responsibility for contributing to the collective expression of a common good.

Having an opportunity to take responsibility for the common good does not guarantee someone will know what to say when the opportunity is given. *Long Night's Journey into Day*, the 2000 documentary of four amnesty cases heard by the TRC, illustrates the point that simply having the opportunity to participate does not by itself provide the rhetorical resources for participation. *Long Night's Journey into Day* gives visual expression to just how difficult it was for amnesty applicants and families of their victims to participate together in dialogues of reconciliation, both formal and informal. The film further suggests how much more difficult reconciliation is outside the constraints imposed by the institutional structure of the TRC.

An obstacle to dialogue in all four cases documented in the film is anonymity or alienation, in particular the emotional distance created between people through apartheid policies. The indifference to another's life—nurtured during the apartheid era, lingering as an obstacle to post-apartheid dialogue—is communicated simply and directly by Neliswa Solatshu, cousin of Mongezi Manqina, one of four young men convicted of the August 25, 1993, murder of American exchange student Amy Biehl, who was chased down and stabbed to death in Gugulethu township. Manqina was a member of the Pan Africanist Student Organisation (PASO). He and the other men convicted in the murder were returning from a PASO rally—where they were incited to violence by the slogan, "one settler, one bullet"—when they found Biehl, pursued her as she fled, and stoned and stabbed her to death. As Solatshu puts it, she didn't care much at first about the death of Amy Biehl, saying about her feelings at the time, "she's a white woman, what the hell do I care about that." Her honesty is chilling, yet her statement is comprehensible. In the final days of apartheid, when so many of her fellow black South Africans were dying violent deaths, after she had lived a lifetime of racial oppression, the death of one white woman would seem less consequential.

While Amy Biehl's parents displayed an extraordinary capacity for forgiveness of their daughter's murderers, traveling to South Africa to meet with their families, *Long Night's Journey into Day* does not address what might compel Solatshu to change her mind and come to care about a person who is white. Yet motivation to change is central to reconciliation. In post-apartheid South Africa, if every person regardless of race is to participate in discussion of a common good, it matters not only that blacks like Solatshu have regard for whites. It matters also that whites such as Sharon Welgemoed cultivate regard for blacks. Welgemoed's sister was killed on June 14, 1986, in Durban by a bomb set by Robert McBride, who joined Umkhonto we Sizwe, the guerilla wing of the ANC, out of frustration with the dehumanizing racism of apartheid. The bomb he planted was intended to kill off-duty security forces. That McBride's bomb killed only three women, one of them Welgemoed's sister, embittered her to the ANC in general and McBride in particular. As she put it, "all he did was contribute to the violence, hatred, and segregation we all wanted to disappear. . . . Mr. McBride is a cold-blooded murderer. He can never wipe away the pain, sorrow, anguish, and destruction he caused."

Solatshu had no regard for Biehl; Welgemoed has no regard for McBride. Their experiences of each other through apartheid oppose them to each other. Solatshu has initially cultivated indifference to whites such as Biehl. Welgemoed has acquired contempt, perhaps even hatred, for blacks such as McBride. Yet it is through these differences that they must find a way toward a common good. As difficult and as painful as it may be for them to reconcile, it is not impossible. As Aristotle explains in *On Rhetoric,* our differences in emotional experience and judgment no doubt require of us that we work to find the words with which to persuade each other (2.1.8); at the same time we recognize it is possible for there to be persuasion because we are social and political beings, beings who need to trust others and who are capable of goodwill and friendliness (2.1.7). The challenge is to find ways and words to cultivate that trust in others.

Through its visualization of four opportunities for reconciliation, *Long Night's Journey into Day* reveals something of the rhetorical resources—both the goodwill and friendliness as well as the emotional pain and experiential differences—available for ordinary South Africans to express their responsibility for the common good. The film presents the faces of reconciliation, faces of ordinary people who have within them the potential for good as well as evil. These are not the high-profile faces of Desmond Tutu, Eugene de Kock, or Winnie Mandela. These are the faces of Neliswa Solatshu and Sharon Welgemoed, people who hurt, people whose hurt threatens to embitter them. But the film's focus on the moment of reconciliation provides the audience only one small part of the larger human experience of being pulled by both a sense of goodwill and the pain of individual experiences that foster feelings of disregard or contempt. For ordinary people like Solatshu and Welgemoed to come to cultivate a shared sense of goodwill requires that they find different expressions for their disregard and contempt. They must find a way past the anguish that closes them off from each other to some feelings that allow them to open themselves to each other.

There can be no one way toward such availability, a point illustrated by the range of post-apartheid South African films that explore the emotional complexity of such personal transformation. These films contribute to the collective expression of a common good by giving audiences rich narrative characterizations of the transformation of experiences of hurt into hope for forgiveness. Two such films, *Tsotsi* and *District 9,* trace the struggle of protagonists coming to terms with indifference and contempt, respectively. In *Tsotsi* the protagonist is black. In *District 9* the protagonist is white. The two films taken together give visual expression to a general understanding of the rhetorical resources black and white South Africans have at their disposal to make themselves available for persuading each other.

In the opening scene of *Tsotsi*, the 2003 film adaptation of Athol Fugard's 1980 novel of the same name, a young African man dressed in black pants, a red shirt, and a black leather jacket leads his gang through the streets of a post-apartheid township. He is leading them to Park Station, the central train station in Johannesburg, where they spot Gumboot Dhlamini who is returning home from work with his pay envelope in the inside pocket of his suit. The gang leader is ultimately leading them to the packed train car where they will rob Dhlamini of his pay and kill him with an ice pick. In the township, on the way to Park Station, the gang of four walk toward the camera, which is focused tightly on the young leader's face. His expression is calculating, emotionless; he stares back at the camera without blinking. His return of the camera's gaze denies his subjection. As the young man strides aggressively toward it, the camera recedes. His arms swinging, he swaggers, his body moving to the rhythm of Zola's "Mdlwembe," a kwaito song with a driving urban beat. The young man is threatening, menacing. He is a wreck of apartheid, a tsotsi.

During the early days of apartheid, tsotsis were the thieves and thugs who preyed on others living in the townships. The tsotsis who victimized others were themselves seen as victims of apartheid, their individual actions explained in terms of a racist system that broke their spirits, robbed them of their humanity, and left them without hope. Robert Sobukwe's challenges to the pass laws were grounded in recognition that state regulation of individual movements displaced and degraded Africans, leaving them, as he concluded, with "broken homes, tsotsis and gangsterism." For the individual subject to apartheid segregation, Moses Dlamini, in *Hell-Hole Robben Island,* his memoir of imprisonment, imagines that being a wreck of apartheid means being "unable to speak coherently—stuttering or with a slur and fearing any White man I come across. And when someone tells of the struggle for freedom—looking at him in shock and just shaking my head" (33).

As Sobukwe argued and Dlamini alluded, there is a causal relationship between tsotsi-ism and apartheid, a relationship which infers that eliminating the cause would eradicate the consequence. Unfortunately the official end of apartheid did not mean an end to the cycle of victimization that is tsotsi-ism. Violent crime persists. Materialists critical of the transition to democracy in South Africa do have a point when they argue that the lingering effects of apartheid—made visually apparent in the violence of the opening scene of *Tsotsi*—are consequences of the persistence of poverty that diminishes the life chances of many black South Africans. Inherent in these criticisms is a suggestion related to but different from Sobukwe's: that improving economic conditions in the townships would to some degree alleviate the anger and frustration that perpetuate tsotsi-ism. Changes in material circumstance would no doubt have a profound effect on the people of South Africa.

But people also experience material circumstances of poverty or affluence emotionally as well as physically. Emotional experiences of deprivation or degradation that made people wrecks of apartheid do not simply disappear from memory when circumstances are improved. To persuade tsotsis to forego violent expression of their anger, bitterness, frustration, and helplessness in the face of systemic victimization requires more than economic reform. Even though one of the lessons of the TRC is that people best confront their victimization through a desire for dialogue, there is no easy rhetoric to which we can appeal to guide such dialogue. Availability and openness to the words people are able to find together to express to each other their experiences of humanity do not exist prior to dialogue. As Gobodo-Madikizela experienced it, finding the appropriate words and being ready to listen to those words comes in the moment of reconciliation itself, through a willingness to take on the risk of self required by caring for and trusting another.

My view throughout this book is that risking care and trust are as foundational to rhetorics of democracy as they are elusive. Something of the nature of such risk drives the narrative of *Tsotsi*, a film which gives visual expression to questions about risking vulnerability in the present after having been victimized and a victimizer in the past. The young man who strides deliberately toward the victimization of Gumboot Dhlamini in the opening scene of the film has few words. He has no name, no character, no memory. He can return the gaze of the camera because the camera does not penetrate him. He is what he appears to be. He is the personification of a wreck of apartheid, he is simply called "Tsotsi."

Drinking in a shabeen (an unlicensed bar) immediately following the robbery and murder of Dhlamini, the character of Tsotsi is confronted by a fellow gang member, Boston, who is visibly shaken by what they have just done. Boston, defensive about his squeamishness, challenges Tsotsi to reveal himself: "What's your name, Tsotsi? Your real name. Tsotsi? Thug? That's not a real name." All the while Tsotsi stares back at Boston with the same unblinking emotionless stare he had prior to Dhlamini's murder. Not getting a response from Tsotsi, Boston continues to challenge the youth: "Decency, Tsotsi. You know the word? I got sick because there's some decency left in me." Breaking a beer bottle on the side of the table, Boston cuts his forearm with the jagged glass, describing his emotional pain with the murder of Dhlamini in terms of the bleeding wound. He asks Tsotsi if anyone ever wounded him so deeply—a lover, his father, his mother, perhaps a dog. At the mention of a dog Tsotsi can no longer hold back his rage. He lunges across the table toward Boston and begins to kick and beat him nearly to death.

Boston lies on the floor, semi-conscious, his face a bloodied pulp. Tsotsi is now the one who is visibly shaken. His emotionless expression is replaced by a look of terror as the patrons of the crowded shabeen stare in disbelief at what he has done to Boston. Tsotsi does bleed; he feels wounded, a wound Boston's words have touched. He runs from the shabeen, frightened. He keeps running across a wide field, during which time a memory returns to him. He remembers himself as a young boy. Images of the young boy, tears streaming down his face, and the young man the boy has become, are intercut as Tsotsi runs scared across a dark field toward an upper-middle-class suburb. Under a tree, in the rain, he recalls another memory from his childhood, huddling with other orphans in a stack of cement sewer pipes, sharing the comforts of little warmth and meager food. In these memories we glimpse his early life, a life of neglect in which the only comfort is shared with others who share in the neglect.

His concentration is broken, and he is recalled to the present by the sound of an approaching car which has pulled up to a security gate in front of a spacious home. As he watches, a woman gets out of the car to call her husband over the gate's intercom because her remote control does not open the gate. Seeing that she has made herself vulnerable, he moves towards the open car door while drawing a gun from his belt. Getting behind the wheel, he begins to drive away, but not without shooting the woman as she tries to stop him. A ways down the road, Tsotsi is startled by the sound of a baby's cries from the back seat of the car, so startled that he has run the car off the road. Tsotsi decides to leave the wreckage and take from it anything of value. As he begins to walk away, the constant sound of the baby's cries stops him. Something about the infant holds his attention and so, before abandoning the wreck, he takes the baby out of its car seat, places it in a paper bag, and carries it away with him.

The scene in the shabeen and the scene on the road signal the beginnings of Tsotsi's experience of himself as something more than a thug. As a gang leader he is cold and calculating in his victimizing of others. He has been without regard for what anyone else might feel. Unlike Boston, he appears to not feel the twinge of his conscience. He simply has no decency. The price he pays to discount his other-regarding emotions is to give up a sense of himself as a person among others. His immediate needs and desires are his primary concern. Someone without decency or conscience, someone without the feelings of shame that follow being seen and judged by others, he has no self. He is a tsotsi. Nothing more than a calculating thief and murderer, he has no guilt, no shame, he has made himself invulnerable. But such invulnerability to oneself and to others is difficult for him to sustain. After Boston confronts him with who he is, after he feels the gaze of the shabeen patrons on him, since he has taken the infant from the car, memories begin returning to him and the audience begins to catch glimpses that Tsotsi is himself someone who was victimized, someone who is vulnerable. To survive the pain of being vulnerable to victimization, he has become the victimizer. Caring for the helpless infant boy begins to change that.

He awakens the next morning in his corrugated metal shack to the sounds and smell of the infant. Ill equipped to care for the baby, he replaces the dirty diaper the infant was wearing and fashions a replacement out of newspapers which he wraps around the child with a scarf. Tsotsi is satisfied with himself that he is able to quiet the baby's hungry cries by dribbling condensed milk into its mouth, and a smile spreads across his face. The contentment of the scene is interrupted as the other members of his gang, Aap and Butcher, bang on his door. To conceal the infant from them, he places the child back in the bag in which it had slept and slides the bag under his bed. Stepping outside to talk with Aap and Butcher, he meets them with the familiar cold, hard stare of impenetrability.

Tsotsi cares for the vulnerable, dependent infant. He also plans to return that night with Aap and Butcher to Park Station to prey on another victim. What sense can we make of this? Tsotsi is himself ambivalent. He conceals the baby from Aap and Butcher, suggesting that he does recognize the incongruity. Maybe he simply does not want to explain himself. But it is most certainly more. The memories aroused in him by the events of the night before are bewildering to him. That he has not yet made himself able to understand the conflict growing in him is made apparent in the next scene, his confrontation with Morris at Park Station.

Tsotsi trips over Morris, a paraplegic in a wheelchair who begs for change from the passengers who rush past him to their destinations. The old man scolds him and spits on his shoe. Tsotsi follows the man as he wheels out of the train station to a secluded area. Feeling threatened, afraid he is going to be robbed of the money he has begged, Morris asks Tsotsi what he wants. All he wants is to know what happened to Morris's legs and why he goes on living when he is crippled like a broken dog. Morris answers that he worked in the mines until a beam fell on him; now he continues to live because he can still take pleasure from the feel of the heat of the sun on the pavement. Tsotsi's interest in Morris is motivated by his own internal conflicts, his struggle to understand what it is to accept the pain of his own victimization as a part of himself that does not consume him. He seems to only know being either the victimized or the victimizer. Both are roles which oppose the self to another, roles in which the sovereignty of a self is asserted through control over another, denying any virtue to vulnerability.

Choosing to take the infant and care for him, Tsotsi has allowed himself to admit the possibility of trusting others without controlling them, although it is not so easy to accept all that such trust entails. Tsotsi realizes he cannot really take care of the infant as he needs to. It is a realization that drives him to force himself upon Miriam, a woman he has seen near the water pump in his township. He follows her home and at gunpoint forces her to breastfeed the infant. At this moment he still acts the only way he knows how, by forcing his will on another. But as he watches Miriam care for the infant, memories of his mother—bedridden and dying from AIDS—return to him, and an awareness wells up inside him that the wall of invulnerability he has built to protect himself is a barrier that separates him from himself. Miriam asks him the child's name. He hesitates for a moment and then recalls his own name. He answers, "David."

With the initial awareness of pleasure in his own need for nurture, David begins a journey of dissociation from his life as a tsotsi. It is not a straightforward or simple journey. He struggles to make amends with Boston by bringing him under his care. He struggles to care for the infant in the only way he knows how, by breaking into the house of the child's parents to acquire food and clothing. Such measures prove not only inadequate; they are inappropriate. His desire to care for the infant is still at this point in the film a desire to exert control over another. He hangs on to the infant because the child serves a purpose, sparking in him a sense that he is more than another wreck of apartheid. As time passes, as desperate as he is to rekindle his experiences of nurture through his care for the infant, David realizes he has neither the capacity nor the resources adequate to the task of caring for another. He also realizes that his interest in caring for the infant is motivated by his desire to understand his own need for nurture, a need which his care for the kidnapped child will not satisfy. He must give up the infant.

In the final scene of *Tsotsi,* David returns to the home from which he stole the car and inadvertently abducted the infant. He is changed, dressed now in a white shirt. His eyes well with tears as the police surround him and the infant's father approaches him in order to retrieve his child. Helpless and weeping, David surrenders the infant to its father; he then surrenders to the police. In this conclusion to the film David's awareness of himself with others manifests itself in the appearance of feelings of regret with what he has done and relief that he can experience within himself a measure of decency. He has no choice but to submit himself to arrest. We are left to presume that he will be convicted for the crimes he has committed, that he will spend many years in prison. There is no doubt he has committed multiple crimes. He has robbed and killed at will, and these crimes cannot go unacknowledged.

Conventions of justice require that he be held accountable for what he has done, but the terms and conditions of accountability are not unambiguous. While his arrest does satisfy a retributive sense of justice, this conclusion to the film is less than satisfying to our sense of restorative justice. What makes it so is the relationship of his self-discovery to his arrest. He had the opportunity to avoid arrest but did not take it. He accepts that he has done wrong. He has come to learn something of the meaning of the word "decency," the word that tormented Boston, the word with which Boston tormented David. But coming to understand what it is to be a decent human being is not enough to excuse what he has done. He willingly surrenders himself to the police. He accepts the demands that justice places on him to pay for his crime. In the end David accepts that decency requires that he accept his fate as a member of society.

It would misrepresent the tragedies of apartheid to focus exclusively on the character of a tsotsi as victim and victimizer, as someone who must come to terms with what it means to be a member of society, someone who must learn how to be vulnerable, who must accept punishment as the price he pays for inclusion. Apartheid was a system of racial classification motivated by insecurities born of exclusion, a desire among Afrikaners to avoid vulnerability at the hands of the British by acquiring absolute sovereignty. The apartheid desire for sovereignty over self and others was created and sustained through a narrative which subsumed conscience and decency to the demands for control. To share in the burden of learning how to be vulnerable to others in a post-apartheid South Africa requires of Afrikaner officials that they find sources for their decency by finding different relationships to others. These themes are explored in *District 9*, a science-fiction film in which problems of xenophobia are explored through the story of extraterrestrials living in a township near Johannesburg.

In *District 9* an Afrikaner, Wikus van der Merwe, works for MNU—Multi National United—a security company that overtly polices the alien township in Johannesburg and covertly researches alien weapons technology. Van der Merwe is awkward and, as his mother says, not very smart. The best word to describe him might be "sniveling." He is a middle manager, a bureaucrat, the kind of person Hume describes as disgusting because he "crouches to his superiors" and is "insolent to his inferiors" (quoted in Miller, 181). At the beginning of *District 9*, van der Merwe is at his desk at work, in a room full of countless other desks, where he fumbles nervously to attach a microphone to the beige sweater vest he wears over a short-sleeved white shirt and thickly knotted brown necktie. He gropes for words in his attempt to explain what he does. His explanation is halting and superficial, insensitive and inappropriate. He uses the word "prawn" to refer to the extraterrestrials MNU is charged with liaising. It is a derogatory term, street slang used by those humans frightened of and repulsed by the extraterrestrials. It is a term that refers with disgust to the crustacean bodily features of those non-humans who have become stranded in Johannesburg. Where humans have mouths, the extraterrestrials have short, thick, dangling tentacles. They crave canned cat food. Their exoskeletal bodies are stained with droppings. On their abdomens are rows of raptorial legs, like those of a praying mantis, that twitch randomly.

Recently promoted to MNU field officer, van der Merwe is charged with relocating the extraterrestrials from the township in which they live to a fenced-in facility 250 kilometers from Johannesburg. Van der Merwe is delighted with the assignment, grateful for the opportunity to prove himself to his superiors. He is also oblivious to his own disgust, although he is proud to put his contempt on display, as when he comments during the burning of alien fetuses that the sound of egg sacks rupturing in the flames echoes the sound of popcorn popping. His xenophobia horrifies and disgusts us. He disgusts his fellow Afrikaners as well, but not because they find his callousness reprehensible.

Koobus Venter, a colonel in MNU security, has only contempt for van der Merwe. Placed temporarily under van der Merwe's command during the alien relocation mission, he assaults and insults van der Merwe for challenging him about being "inefficient" because he and his men are carrying too much ammunition into the township. Venter is an intimidating figure, and he has no patience for van der Merwe. His features are hard, his movements decisive, his speech curt, his gaze direct and calculating. Van der Merwe, on the other hand, is easily intimidated by Venter. He is weak. His features are soft, his movements clumsy, his speech rambling, and his gaze unfocused. He would not have been put in charge of the relocation of the extraterrestrials if his father-in-law, Piet Smit, was not managing director of MNU South Africa. Smit himself appears as hard-nosed as Venter. He is clean cut, trim, emotionless, and calculating. He too has no fondness for van der Merwe, who is for Smit nothing more than a means to an end.

We easily imagine Smit and Venter as descendants of the Vortrekkers, hearty and stalwart pioneers who, in the 1830s, migrated inland from the southern Cape to escape British rule and settle the rugged interior. We can imagine van der Merwe less as a Vortrekker, less a proud Afrikaner settler, and more as a city dweller, one of the many poor Afrikaners who migrated to the urban centers of South Africa during the 1920s, illiterate laborers looking for work but finding little more than poverty and degradation because they had to compete for jobs with black Africans who could be made by the British to work harder for less pay.

The exclusion of Afrikaner farmers and laborers from economic and political power in British South Africa motivated a secret society of Afrikaner leaders, the Broederbond, to work toward the goal of establishing the national sovereignty of Afrikaner racial and cultural identity. Their goal was realized in 1948 when the National Party won parliamentary elections, at which point they began passing laws aimed at total separation of white South Africans from all South Africans of color. Motivated by the embitterment of their own experiences of ethnic exclusion, the members of the Broederbond were unrelenting in their pursuit of the sovereign national identity of Afrikaners. The architect of apartheid policies, Hendrik Verwoerd, made clear his indifference to anything but the full actualization of apartheid in South Africa when he explained in an interview, "I don't believe in a policy of conciliation. I believe in a policy of conviction" (Giliomee, 519). The cost of holding to apartheid convictions was paid in large measure by those South Africans of color forcibly relocated from their homes and communities to distant areas designated as their homelands.

One of the most notorious relocations took place over a span of almost twenty years in an area of Cape Town known as District Six. As with apartheid policies in general, the forced relocations of the residents of District Six aroused in many South Africans feelings of anger, contempt, despair, and disgust. After District Six residents had been displaced, the land—vacated of people and of the dwellings they occupied—remained undeveloped because the forced relocations were so blatantly shameful. After the end of apartheid, efforts began to find former residents and return them to the area they used to call home.

In democratic South Africa, District Six symbolizes the inviolability of human character refusing to give way to the demands of regulation and systemization (Marback, *A Tale*).

Crouching to his superiors and insolent to his inferiors, Van der Merwe commits himself unquestioningly to regulating the task of relocating extraterrestrials from District 9. He is eager to please men like Venter and Smit, men whose demeanor recalls the figure of Verwoerd. During the relocation campaign, supported by Venter's security forces, Van der Merwe goes door to door in District 9 serving eviction notices. It does not go smoothly. In his clumsy handling of a cylinder he has found in his search of a makeshift dwelling, van der Merwe is sprayed in the face with a black fluid. Frustrated and sickened, he loses patience with an alien who refuses to sign an eviction notice. The alien attacks him, and van der Merwe is wounded in the hand. Slowly, but perceptibly, the contamination from the black spray takes its toll. Black fluid starts dripping from his nose. He begins vomiting. That night, in the middle of a party celebrating his promotion, he vomits viscous black fluid on a cake he is cutting for his guests, after which he loses consciousness. At the hospital, as a physician cuts the bandage away from his hand, van der Merwe is horrified to see the metamorphosis of his fingers into large crustacean-like claws.

Where van der Merwe had been an object of contempt and disgust to his fellow Afrikaners, he was now, because of his metamorphosed alien appendage, of particular interest to Smit and MNU. Van der Merwe, horrified and contaminated, is transformed from an object of disgust to an object of interest because Smit sees an opportunity to use him to make functional the captured extraterrestrial weaponry that only alien bodies can operate. Strapped to a gurney, van der Merwe is wheeled into a research facility dripping with the vivisected remains of aliens. As Smit looks on, tight lipped, unblinking, van der Merwe's body is mercilessly tortured in an effort to make functional the captured alien weaponry. When it is realized that van der Merwe's DNA allows him to unlock and fire the extraterrestrial weapons, the decision is made to harvest his body parts and extract the DNA, or, as the lead researcher puts it, "harvest material from the specimen." Because van der Merwe is more valuable dead than alive, Smit tells his distraught daughter that her husband (who is not yet dead) has died from his wounds, consoling her by explaining to her that he "never was very strong."

We are meant to feel horrified with, to be revolted by, the heartless treatment van der Merwe receives. The behavior of MNU executives and scientists is viscerally wrenching. We are disgusted with their inability to feel disgust. Steely, clinical, undeterred—blind to the blood and gore of the butchered flesh strewn around them, deaf to the whimpering pleas of their victim—they proceed with their plan to extract the still-beating heart from the chest of a conscious van der Merwe. These are people who have lost the capacity to respect the dignity of human life. These are people who have hardened themselves against feeling disgust with anything they themselves might think or want or do.

The MNU technician who shocks van der Merwe in the arm with a cattle prod in order to make him fire the alien weapon understands that van der Merwe suffers. He seems to not feel pity for his victim. He seems to simply not care. He intends for van der Merwe to suffer. Yet we do not feel sympathy for him either. We do not feel compassion for the man who has taken pleasure in the sound of alien fetuses rupturing in the flames. Feeling pity, experiencing someone else's suffering as undeserved, is different from feeling sympathy, or compassion, for the person who suffers.

To be sympathetic to the suffering of another is to do more than comprehend, as the torturer surely does, that another is suffering. It is also to feel more than pity for someone who we understand is suffering undeservedly. To feel sympathy is to somehow experience the pain of another's suffering as something more than an undeserved wrong. As Aristotle observes in his definition of pity, we often express the experience of another's suffering by saying that we "know what it is like" to feel loss or pain because we ourselves have had—or can easily imagine—similar experiences. This kind of identification is necessary for sympathy, but it is not sufficient. I can identify with someone's suffering by saying I know what it is like to have that experience, all the while thinking to myself it isn't as bad as all that. Genuine sympathy seems to require sensitivity to the fact that someone else's suffering is as bad as she says it is. The other's experience of suffering must concern us. It must touch us.

To be concerned for and touched by another's suffering demands of us vulnerability, an openness to the possibility of being wounded by our experience of the suffering of another. As Nussbaum makes clear, such vulnerability is the product of intimacy. The compassion we feel for someone is not just a recognition of suffering and of the suffering being undeserved; it is also that the person who suffers matters to us, that we value their well being as an end in itself (Nussbaum, 321). When someone else's well being becomes a goal for us, that person becomes part of our primary concern. Sympathy for a person who matters, whose suffering therefore matters, can lead us to momentarily put aside those things we aspired to prior to our learning of that person's pain. When sympathy is so great, as when parents care for their terminally ill child, nothing else does matter. To be sympathetic is to open oneself to the prospect of such all-consuming concern. It is to accept the inevitability of what George Harris has called benign integral breakdown, a strength of character expressed through our regard for others, which makes us vulnerable to the pain of the loss of those relationships, a loss that disrupts our personal integrity by threatening to take away from us a person who has figured in our primary concerns.

The parents who care for their terminally ill child do so because they love and value and are committed to a person whose well being matters, and so whose suffering matters, a person who (despite their best efforts) will soon be gone from their lives, a loss they anticipate, and accept, and will experience as a diminishment of themselves. As Harris explains, "There is overwhelming evidence that those who cope best with tragedy befalling loved ones are those who are involved in healthy personal relationships that are deeply intimate, even though it is this kind of intimacy that made tragedy possible in the first place" (131). To be sympathetic is to intimately experience another's needs as our own in a way that cannot but threaten to tragically disrupt our personal integrity. Depending on the degree of another's suffering, and depending on our commitment to the other's well being as an end integral to our own lives, we feel a loss to ourselves in the other's pain.

It is important to recall that sympathy is concern for another person's suffering. However deeply pained we may feel by the suffering of someone we care about, our concern remains with the other person whose pain and suffering is her own. Nussbaum summarizes it this way: "compassion makes thought attend to certain human facts, and in a certain way, with concern to make the lot of the suffering person as good, things being equal, as it can be—because that person is an object of one's concern." She adds, drawing from Aristotle's definition of emotions such as pity, that such concern is never completely altruistic: "Often that concern is motivated or supported by the thought that one might oneself be, one day, in that person's position" (342). While it may well be that people are often motivated to concern themselves with another's suffering out of an awareness that they themselves might someday suffer the same fate, such accounts of self-regard tend to overstate the extent of self-interest by presuming that people are, for the most part, not in the vulnerable position of suffering and so not normally in need of another's compassion.

Alternatively, Bryan Turner has described the human experience of need as well as capacity for sympathy in terms of the everyday precariousness and vulnerability of our mortal existence: "As an aspect of human frailty, our ontological vulnerability includes the idea that human beings of necessity have an organic propensity to disease and sickness, that death and dying are inescapable, and that aging bodies are subject to impairment and disability. The human life cycle is characterized by its finite possibilities (and is thus inescapably tragic).

Because of these conditions, human beings are involved in various relationships of dependency throughout the life cycle" (29). Sympathy, an emotion we cultivate out of our dependence on others, does not provide escape from our dependency. Rather, it is through our dependence on, and so sympathy for, each other that we are able to pursue our well being. The virtue of sympathy, then, is not that it functions as a kind of categorical imperative promoting a norm of reciprocal regard. Sympathy, rather, is a condition of our awareness of ourselves among others. Through our sympathy we are able to consider the well being of others as integral to our own well being, and so our striving for our goals cannot but take others and their goals into account.

Smit or the other MNU employees are not sympathetic, and still they do experience disgust. They have cultivated a sense of themselves as not disgusting because those things which are disgusting are kept apart from themselves. The bodies of the extraterrestrials are held at a safe distance. Unlike the Nigerian gang leader who eats the flesh of aliens in the hopes of ingesting their powers, the employees of MNU are more cultivated—they are above such primitive witchcraft. Their control of the machines in the research facility make them impenetrable to the bloody extraterrestrial remains, van der Merwe's cries, anything that threatens to contaminate them.

The aspiration to void oneself of the disgusting is an aspiration to control absolutely, to make impenetrable, the boundaries of the self. Such control extends beyond the self, necessarily involving the isolation of others who are reviled, others who, as objects of revulsion, secure the self from its own loathing. There is in this critical understanding of the denial of disgust a presumption of the need for accepting some measure of disgust, at least with oneself, at least enough to guarantee the kind of humility necessary for respecting the dignity of others. At the same time, however, allowing some measure of self-loathing and revulsion, allowing ourselves to experience our animal bodies and visceral natures, gives us no guarantee of humility and little guidance in our interactions with others. We know, for example, that judgments justified in terms of appeal to experiences of disgust often denigrate others, and so a morality based on disgust gives us no assurance that we are consistently respecting the dignity of others.

Sympathy, as an acceptance of one's own neediness and the neediness of others, provides a potential restraint on disgust. To function as emotionally healthy people we need to feel sympathy as well as disgust. We need to tolerate, as Otto Kernberg puts it, "a realistic view of the self as potentially imbued with both loving and hating impulses," a view which makes it possible to have "integrated, ambivalent relationships with others in contrast to splitting them into idealized and persecutory objects" (10). As people who feel disgust and sympathy and a whole range of often contradictory emotions, we must somehow keep our disgust from getting the better of our sympathy while keeping our sympathy from burying our disgust. As Kernberg puts it, "The normal personality is characterized, first of all, by an integrated concept of the self and an integrated concept of significant others. . . . An integrated view of one's self assures the capacity for a realization of one's desires, capacities, and long-range commitments. An integrated view of significant others guarantees the capacity for an appropriate evaluation of others, empathy, and an emotional investment in others that implies a capacity for mature dependency while maintaining a consistent sense of autonomy" (8).

Where at the beginning of *District 9* van der Merwe had been an object of the disgust to his Afrikaner superiors, someone who in turn made the stranded extraterrestrials objects of his disgust, he becomes upon his metamorphosis an object of his own disgust and pity. As the audience, we are persuaded that the disgust we have been encouraged to experience can lead us to greater respect for the dignity of others, and we come to feel sympathy for someone who has disgusted us. We were introduced to van der Merwe as morally disgusting through his contempt for extraterrestrials. As he acquires visceral disgust for himself, as he is treated by his superiors in morally disgusting ways, we are encouraged to feel pity for him. At this point our pity is not sympathy. He may not deserve the treatment he gets, but he also does not yet deserve our compassion, in large part because our disgust over his treatment of the extraterrestrials still lingers. His body has been transformed, but he is morally not much different from those who torture him. Until he reveals himself as able to experience within himself not only feelings of disgust but also of sympathy, we cannot regard him with anything more than pity.

If aversion to disgust is the way to fascism, and if deference to disgust is the way to narrow moralism, then integrating appeals to disgust with appeals to sympathy is required for relationships in which people can come to respect the dignity and integrity of each other. For such an ambivalent alternative to be viable, van der Merwe must somehow relinquish the power of his disgust with himself for sympathy for another. This is not to say he must replace disgust with sympathy. What he must do is accept the integrity of his feelings of disgust and sympathy. He must accept that both feelings are part of his experience of himself among others. I think the transformation of van der Merwe's disgust, as it tracks his metamorphosis to the conclusion of the film, points in the direction of such a non-idealized, ambivalent integration of self and other.

While Smit's aversion to disgust becomes more and more viscerally disturb-ing as we watch him treat his son-in-law as little more than meat, van der Merwe's disgust with himself, as well as his desire for the comfort of his own integrity, becomes more comprehensibly familiar. Driven by fear for his own survival, van der Merwe manages to escape the facility where he has been imprisoned and tortured. To facilitate his capture MNU televises bulletins accusing van der Merwe of having intercourse with extraterrestrials. Not only is his behavior portrayed as disgusting, he is described as contagious and in need of immediate capture and isolation. As a result, people run from him. He cannot, however, escape the self he has become. He too finds himself disgusting, not because he is a miscegenist (which he is not), not because he is contagious (which he is not), but because he is ostracized. He simply wants to return to a prior, uncontami-nated, not-disgusting self that had the unconditional affirmation of his wife's love. What pains him most is not his disgust with himself—it is that the charac-terizations of him as disgusting make him repugnant to his wife.

Despite his desires to somehow reverse his contamination, his crustacean appendage consumes his flesh. He begins to crave canned cat food. Despite his attempt to whack his hand off with an ax, he is irrevocably contaminated, he is ostracized, he is changed. His disgust with the metamorphosis of his own body only grows. He simply wants to escape his disgust and return to his wife. In his desperate flight he stumbles across an extraterrestrial, Christopher John-son, who explains that he can reverse the metamorphosis once they retrieve from MNU the black fluid-filled canister which originally contaminated van der Merwe. Initially he treats the extraterrestrial with contempt, calling him a "prawn," and demanding that the alien return him to "normal." Reluctantly, van der Merwe accepts that, if he is to secure the assistance of Johnson, he must at least restrain his disgust.

In search of the canister, the two break into the MNU research facility, where Christopher Johnson sees the eviscerated bodies of his kin who had been the subjects of medical experiments. He is sickened and saddened. In a moment of recognition, van der Merwe feels sympathy, but it is fleeting. The only consola-tion he can offer is that, until he had himself become the subject of experimen-tation, he too didn't know. Recognizing the threat of genocide, Johnson decides he must first use the canister to save his people before he helps van der Merwe reverse his metamorphosis. This is a decisive moment for van der Merwe. He needs Johnson, who has decided he must first return to his home planet to secure help for his people, a mission that he says will require van der Merwe to wait three years. Of course three years is too long to wait. A little less than three days has passed and, as the metamorphosis spreads across his back, van der

Merwe already tears painfully at his own flesh in a vain attempt to secure what little is left of his bodily integrity.

Eventually, to some degree, van der Merwe must accept his fate. He must embrace his disgust with himself. His decision is neither easy nor straightforward. His own desire to return to his wife compels him more than the nonhuman genocide. His fear drives him to try to use the canister to cure himself. The attempt ends disastrously, with van der Merwe's being captured by the Nigerian gang leader who is intent on eating his flesh and Johnson's being captured by Venter's security forces. Moments from death, van der Merwe is saved by Johnson's young son. The youth's compassion compels van der Merwe to finally stop acting out of a desire to rid himself of the contagion, to face his fear of Venter and rescue Christopher Johnson, who is about to be assassinated after being brutally interrogated. During the rescue Van der Merwe, in control of a lethal extraterrestrial weapon, guards Johnson from MNU security so that he can be reunited with his young son. As the pair make their way to the alien escape vessel, van der Merwe narrowly escapes death. He has willingly sacrificed himself for another. Broken and bloodied, he watches in vain as Johnson and his son ascend into the atmosphere, leaving him behind to complete his metamorphosis.

District 9 concludes with Wikus van der Merwe's wife twirling a small flower fashioned out of scraps of metal. She opines that the flower, which she found one day on her doorstep, had been crafted and left there by her husband, who is missing, and who, as his father flatly explains, "died in my mind a long time ago. And that's that." The closing shot suggests otherwise, focusing on a lone alien, standing in a pile of refuse, intent on the small metal flower he is deliberately, clumsily shaping with his oversized claws.

For Wikus van der Merwe—as for *Tsotsi*'s David—self-discovery changes awareness of oneself among others. Van der Merwe discovers through his physical metamorphosis that his desire for the love of his wife is not unlike Christopher Johnson's desire for a return to his home. The revulsion van der Merwe originally felt for Johnson and his people is revealed to him, through his painful physical transformation, to be a product of the narrow self-interest available to him through his position at MNU. What he realizes after it is too late is that the executives at MNU care only about unlocking the secrets of extraterrestrial weapons technology. Prior to his realization, van der Merwe eagerly approaches the task of relocating extraterrestrials, an eagerness that speaks less to his knowledge of and commitment to the company's directives and more to his discomfort with his own insecurity. His role at MNU gave him the opportunity to experience himself as an authority, to aspire to the single-mindedness of

Smit and Venter, an opportunity and ambition which he believed would secure for him the comfort of a future with his wife. What he learns instead is that the resolve of men like Smit and Venter runs counter to the feelings of passion that matter most to him. Smit and Venter are callous. They cannot understand what the extraterrestrial Christopher Johnson understands, that people deny their feelings at the cost of their humanity.

For his part, David discovers through his emotional upheaval that he has denied himself by denying his capacity for care and concern. That he was able to bury for so long his longing for an experience of nurture reflects the depth of anger and hurt he felt in response to denials of nurture in his childhood. Forced at a young age to fend for himself in the townships surrounding Johannesburg, David developed a capacity for disregard that allowed him to experience others as nothing more than a means to his own ends. He personified a tsotsi, a wreck of apartheid. In a society organized around the idea that indifference to others can be justified on the grounds of racial identification, David learns how little he matters to others. He learns as well a disregard for others. These lessons he has learned are at odds with his potential for decency. Confronted with innocence, confronted with the complete dependence of an infant, David is confronted with his capacity for decency. For the first time since he was himself a dependent child, David lets down his defenses and discovers his capacity to experience the joys as well as the sorrows of human life.

For both characters, David and van der Merwe, personal transformation turns on letting go of feelings which justified closing the self off from others while acquiring or developing feelings which encourage openness to the presence of others. For neither character is the transformation easy. At the end of each film the protagonist stands alone, each having surrendered himself to his fate. We would not say that either character is as confident or comfortable or complacent as he was at the start of his story. Both characters are instead freed from the ambitions which distorted their views of themselves and of others. They are both just beginning their lives as vulnerable beings among other vulnerable beings. Their beginnings are fraught with difficulties, and neither character is where he would like to be. David is under arrest. Van der Merwe is metamorphosed and estranged.

At the same time, both characters have affirmed something about themselves. David finds in himself memories of fear and deprivation and longing that awaken in him a sensitivity to others, even as he is led to surrender himself to what we are left to imagine as his imprisonment. In his case the demands of justice are indifferent to the circumstances which crippled his chances in life. Van der Merwe resigns himself to his metamorphosis. He is led to the realization that he is not an Afrikaner. He must find his way alone, excluded by the very racial identifications to which he once aspired. It is an experience of simultaneous alienation and discovery available to Afrikaners such as Rian Malan—a descendent of the Vortrekkers who settled the interior of South Africa to escape British rule—at the end of apartheid: "Strange terrors and ecstacies awaited us in Africa, but that was the choice we faced: Either we stayed where we were, trapped inside our fortress of paranoia, deformed by fear and greed, or we opened the door to Africa and set forth into the unknown" (347).

The self-discoveries of van der Merwe and David reveal possibilities that exist for individual South Africans to see themselves and others differently and so to engage others differently. Their self-discoveries, however, also expose the limitations to seeing and engaging others differently. Conventions of legal justice demand that David surrender himself to the police. Conventions of racial intolerance force van der Merwe to live in isolation. *District 9* and *Tsotsi* visualize our sense that the limits of the possibilities for engaging each other differently are found in the intertwining of individual self-awareness with the social structure of relationships. In both films, narratives of a common good challenge the protagonists with choices that must lead to loss. In *Tsotsi* in particular, the issue of justice is an issue of who is made to carry responsibility. It is worth recalling Pumla Gobodo-Madikizela's response to the proposed presidential pardon for Eugene de Kock. Bystanders and beneficiaries, as well as the perpetrators and victims of apartheid must acknowledge their part in the structuring of human antipathies and sympathies. Together with *Long Night's Journey into Day*, *District 9* and *Tsotsi* communicate to audiences beyond the borders of South Africa just how fragile those narratives of the common good really are.

Chapter 8

THE PROSPECTS OF RHETORIC
AS VULNERABILITY

David's vulnerability leads to his arrest. Wikus van der Merwe's vulnerability leads him to isolation. The fates of these characters are more than fiction. They are characterizations of life in a country where the people are bound by the task of making sense of their present lives together in terms of their past lives apart. The narratives of David and Wikus van der Merwe give expression to the ongoing experience of social availability in post-apartheid South Africa, an experience of emotions such as shame and disgust, compassion and longing, which shape awareness of the self among others. These are also the emotions aroused so intensely in confrontations during the TRC hearings between such perpetrators as Robert McBride or Mongezi Manqina and their victims' family members, Sharon Welgemoed or Amy Biehl's parents. They are the emotions felt by Eugene de Kock and Pumla Gobodo-Madikizela, emotions felt in the physical presence of others, emotions difficult to put into words. While the emotional intensity of encounters structured by the TRC cannot be sustained—if for no other reason than that it would prove exhausting—the characterizations of David and Wikus van der Merwe remind us that the narrative trajectories of human lives—the stories people tell to convince themselves of their sovereignty—arouse in others sensitivities to being vulnerable among others.

In general, sensitivities to ourselves among others give guidance to our persuasive appeals. These sensitivities, as well as the appeals which they ground, compel us in often contradictory directions. On the one hand, disgust and shame and other similar emotions give us a sense of the limits of our sovereignty, revealing to us the contingency of our lives, and making it possible for us to approach others with humility. On the other hand, the pain of disgust and shame more often than not drive us to do whatever we can to make ourselves feel as well as seem to others to be invulnerable to contingency. Clinging to a sense of invulnerability to dull the pain of disgust or shame makes it that much harder for us to appeal honestly and listen openly to others with whom we are bound to discuss those things that are most important, those things that most divide us even as we are bound to live together.

The transition in South Africa from apartheid to democracy tracks across the contradictory impulses to the experience of vulnerability, from an aspiration to sovereignty motivated by fear of exposure to recognition of the experience of vulnerability as fundamental to expressions of sovereignty. Beginning with an account of the rhetoric of Robert Sobukwe and ending with the fictional depictions of David and Wikus Van der Merwe, I have characterized the struggle against apartheid as a challenge to move beyond divisiveness born of Afrikaner ambitions for invulnerability. The legacy of Robben Island, debate over the proposed Freedom Monument, and the rhetoric of the TRC reveal the difference between language critical of invulnerable sovereignty and language struggling to give expression to what I have characterized as sovereign vulnerability—a capacity for rhetorical agency grounded in openness to the anger and antagonism, frailty and suffering, hope and joy of others.

Finally, the films *Tsotsi* and *District 9* give visual representations of characters and relationships in post-apartheid South Africa that reflect the degree to which a viable alternative to the divisiveness of invulnerable sovereignty— sovereign vulnerability—is a deeply emotional experience for which full expression is difficult at best. The conclusion we can take away from observing the still emerging rhetoric of vulnerability can be rather pessimistic in much the same way critics of the TRC have been pessimistic that avowals of reconciliation provided anything in the way of much needed material reparations and restitution for South Africa's most desperate citizens. If we join the ambivalence of *Tsotsi* and *District 9* to the criticisms of the compromises of the TRC, we may be forced to admit that grounding democracy in heightened awareness of dependence and vulnerability asks too much of people, leaving them to resign themselves in their self-awareness to disappointment with demands placed on them by pressures of convention.

The trajectory of South African politics since the end of Mandela's term as president provides fuel to the fires of such skepticism. Mandela's successor, Thabo Mbeki, presided over a country in which the trajectory of the rhetoric of vulnerability has foundered, in large part in response to the AIDS epidemic. In a country in which 320,000 citizens died of HIV-related illnesses in 2005, Mark Gevisser asked, "how was it possible that, at the very moment they assumed their victourious place as the leaders of a democracy they had struggled for decades to bring about, they were presented with a dying populace, with a plague to which there were no answers? This was the era of birth of democracy, of the emergence of a life-force out of the cadaver of apartheid, and yet here were portents that the fear of death—rather than the celebration of life—would drive the country into the future" (278). Questions regarding the relationship between the struggle against apartheid and the struggle against AIDS are questions directed not only at the Mbeki administration, they are questions asking how best to manage the ambitions of sovereignty and the stigmas of vulnerability when those ambitions and stigmas share roots in the constancy of human suffering.

For his part, Mbeki was not indifferent to the ravages of AIDS. His attention to the disease was directed through his sensitivity to the legacy of apartheid. In a speech given at Fort Hare University on October 12, 2001, Mbeki expressed what has been described as an AIDS dissident view, saying in part, "Convinced that we are but natural-born, promiscuous carriers of germs, unique in the world, they proclaim that our continent is doomed to an inevitable mortal end because of our unconquerable devotion to the sin of lust" (quoted in Forrest and Streak). According to this view, proposals to treat HIV/AIDS in Africa exclusively through pharmaceuticals are proposals which stigmatize black Africans by characterizing them as promiscuous. Mbeki assigns the stigma of promiscuity to the failure among European pharmaceutical manufacturers to acknowledge contributions made to the African AIDS epidemic by colonial conquest and apartheid racism.

Anti-retroviral drugs, by themselves, are not in this view the proper response to a disease which disproportionately affects black South Africans whose disenfranchisement has made them the most vulnerable members of society. Sensitivity to race in public health issues such as the AIDS epidemic is part of awareness of all too recent apartheid health policies designed in part to control the fertility of black South Africans (Schneider and Fassin, 49). As became clear during the TRC hearings, the apartheid government had international cooperation—from countries including the United States—in conducting research into chemical and biological weapons intended to "cause disease and undermine the health of communities" (*Truth and Reconciliation Commission of South Africa Report* 2: 510). In light of the history of racism on the African continent and in South Africa, the idea of treating HIV/AIDS as a problem of an individual's responsible sexual behavior—to be addressed through safe-sex public health campaigns and treatable through prescription medication—is an idea that neglects just how complex a public policy issue AIDS is. For one thing, the idea that AIDS is best treated through medicines only available through multinational drug companies raises suspicions regarding the costs of those medications, their availability to the poorest of the poor, as well as the profits to be made by drug manufacturers and distributors. Developing a policy for the distribution of anti-retroviral drugs in South Africa invokes questions about the country's dependence on multinational corporations, its global interdependence, as well as its national independence.

As president of South Africa, Mbeki pursued an initial policy towards HIV/ AIDS that denied anti-retroviral drugs to hundreds of thousands of South Africans as the administration became entangled with issues of sovereignty (Chigwedere). His policy evolved through antagonisms between the government, AIDS activists, and pharmaceutical companies struggling over African autonomy in South Africa. As Gevisser summarizes it, "For Mbeki, the quest for self-determination over health—the legacy of the AIDS epidemic in the West— became confused with the quest for political self-determination" (288). The confusion, according to Gevisser, grounds in Mbeki's sensitivity to the stigma attached to African sexuality, a sense of shame he worked to evade through a materialist understanding of sovereignty: "If we are dying [from HIV/AIDS] because we have too little (or too much, too quickly), then Mbeki's mission—the ANC's rasion d'être—prevails. If, however, we are dying because we cannot control our primal urges, Mbeki's own liberatory paradigm is shattered. We are the Africans whom our colonial oppressors said that we were, and we have not been able to liberate ourselves from their definition of us" (296). Having opposed economics to emotions, Mbeki's rhetoric precludes productive expression of liberation in terms of the intertwining of material sovereignty with emotional vulnerability.

While Gevisser makes a compelling case for understanding Mbeki's AIDS dissident views within the struggle for liberation from colonial rule, it would be inaccurate to suggest that Mbeki's opposition to pharmaceutical companies profiting from the South African AIDS epidemic was consistent with a general antagonism towards capitalism. The South African government has instead encouraged economic growth as a means to revive a country—rich in mineral resources—that had suffered from international sanctions during apartheid. Such policies bring the government into conflict with South African trade unions as well as with more radical leaders such as ANC youth leader Julius Malema, who, in 2009, launched a campaign calling for the nationalization of mines. While Malema remains at odds with the ANC over his continued challenges to party orthodoxy, he has grown in influence because he speaks to a younger generation impatient with the progress of post-apartheid restitution.

Maurice Carney, executive director of Friends of the Congo, commented on Malema's influence in Southern Africa in an October 18, 2011, interview on Afrobeat Radio: "So, this is something to look out for in the coming years, where young people, you know, we see it . . . in North Africa it's reflected, in Tunisia and Egypt, but in Southern Africa we already see the South African youth calling for a greater ownership of their own wealth which they're not benefitting from" ("Resource Sovereignty"). Carney's admiration for Malema is consistent with his disdain for the South African government's post-apartheid economic policies, which he characterizes as a continuation of apartheid policies.

He invokes Naomi Klein's *The Shock Doctrine*—and her view that capitalism is spread through the exploitation of peoples stunned by large-scale disasters—to explain dissatisfaction with the rise of a black elite in South Africa despite the persistent poverty of the majority of black South Africans. Drawing on Klein, Carney explains that the ANC's neoliberalism was affirmed by Mbeki, "because he was primarily responsible for negotiating some of the economic dynamics at the time, that there wouldn't be any radical change. For example, the ANC wouldn't hold to the tenets of its charter, which called for resource sovereignty." He continued, "Even after Mandela and after Mbeki, when Jacob Zuma, who was supposed to be more of a populist . . . was going to come to power, he had talks with companies at the time like Merrill Lynch and reassured the financial markets that under his leadership there wouldn't be any radical changes in the economic order" ("Resource Sovereignty").

Here Carney has appealed to resource sovereignty—the idea of people controlling the wealth of their own nation—to remedy the vulnerabilities of disease, poverty, and unemployment wrought by capitalism. His appeal is not so radically different from Mbeki's. It is rather typical of broader debates regarding who is responsible for, and how best to respond to, a legacy of underdevelopment in Africa. These debates consistently pit neoliberal, or European, approaches to socialist, or African, approaches. Like Carney's appeal, such debates turn on understanding sovereignty and vulnerability in terms of access to and control over material resources. Rhetorics opposing neoliberal to socialist are prevalent among Africanists, and this opposition privileges aspirations for sovereignty over experiences of vulnerability, as the Mbeki administration's policy debate over AIDS sadly demonstrates.

Debates regarding the collective or individual ownership of wealth are largely about competing self-interests. They are debates framed—for better or for worse—through rhetorics that equate command of wealth with a capacity for self-realization. Such a framing fails to allow for constraints on individuals that are not wholly matters of ownership of resources. This point is made evident by the furor over the South African government's delay in granting a tourist visa to the Dalai Lama so that he could travel to Cape Town to celebrate Archbishop Desmond Tutu's eightieth birthday. The government's delay—which led the Dalai Lama to cancel his visit—appears to reflect an interest in nurturing improved trade relations with China at the expense of freedoms won through the struggle against apartheid. As University of Witwatersrand Vice-Chancellor Loyiso Nongxa observed, "The state's deliberate indecision ridicules the values pertaining to freedom of speech, expression and movement enshrined in our Constitution and the freedoms for which so many South Africans have lived, and indeed died." Similarly, the Congress of South African Trade Unions (COSATU) issued a statement concluding, "Even though China is our biggest trading partner, we should have not exchanged our morality for dollars or yuan" (Tsering).

For his part, Tutu publicly admonished the Zuma government: "You represent your own interest and I am warning you, I am really warning you—out of love—I am warning you like I warned the nationalists, one day we will start praying for the defeat of the ANC government" (Davids and Malefane). Whether or not the government's delay was intentional, the incident shows us how easily perceptions of economic interest can come to dominate an issue. A debate that opposes competing interests in terms of a command of economic resources occludes the extent to which the issue at hand is not simply economic. Freedom and morality are not measured solely in terms of who controls what percentage of the wealth. This is not to say the distribution of wealth does not matter in questions of what is good and just, in South Africa as much as anywhere else. Rather, it is to say that productive deliberation regarding competing corporate and individual as well as private and public interests are not had when people on all sides are unable to acknowledge their relationship to the vulnerability of others.

We would be mistaken to conclude from the current situation in South Africa that the rhetorics developed by Sobukwe and Mandela and Tutu and the countless others who struggled against apartheid coalesced in an appeal bound to a discrete time and place. Yet it is not difficult to lose sight of their larger ambition for a better means of managing lives lived with others. In light of the issues and contentions that preoccupy South African politicians today—including but not limited to AIDS, freedom of the press and of movement, government transparency, and wealth redistribution—we could easily view David's arrest in *Tsotsi* and van der Merwe's isolation in *District 9* as prescient visualizations of vulnerabilities to the dehumanizing effects of intractable material inequality. Witnessing the inequalities that persist despite the South African transition to democracy, we could easily resign ourselves to accept that irreconcilable differences are inextricably intertwined with the unfairness of circumstances—not only in South Africa, but anywhere people must decide their fates together. Disappointment with responses such as those of Mbeki or Zuma can motivate resignation that our appeals to each other are more often than not weighted with anxiety over our own sovereignty.

I am more hopeful about the prospects for a rhetoric of vulnerability. The prospects for a rhetoric of the common good are not realized simply by extending to all the opportunity for participation in shared deliberations. There is more. Some measure of vulnerability is an inevitable part of any deliberation about a common good. If we are to take part in deliberations, we must at least accept the prospects of acquiescence, compromise, and defeat. We must also do more. Accepting a measure of vulnerability involves more than resigning ourselves to the limits of our rhetorical capacities. While everyone at one time or another will experience disappointment with deliberations, we constrain our participation if we cynically conclude that disappointment is inevitable as the price to be paid for hope in a common good. Some find the cost too high. My view is that the refusal to risk disappointment costs more. The greater loss is not acquiescence, compromise, or defeat; the greater loss is the loss of opportunities to elaborate shared public lives.

South Africans have struggled to articulate something like a common good out of the realization that the common good cannot be defined once and for all, that decisions about how best to live lives together demand of individuals vulnerabilities to circumstance and exposure to each other. Aspirations for sovereignty and experiences of vulnerability have circulated through recent South African culture, from the Sharpeville massacre to the TRC and beyond. The experiences of vulnerability are not primarily or even exclusively the vulnerabilities of disenfranchisement that persist as the legacy of apartheid, although the ravages of disease, homelessness, malnutrition, and poverty are daily the experience of far too many South Africans. As the tragic legacy of apartheid, these strains on human thriving grab our attention and call for resolution. We best respond to the suffering of others by giving expression to vulnerability in our aspirations for a common good. Being vulnerable is fundamental to the human condition. We can never eliminate it. We must try our best to not ignore it in the experiences of others.

The vulnerabilities I have discussed are vulnerabilities of human experience: victimization by pass laws, preservation of painful memories, acceptance of anguish, disgust, and shame. While the experiences are associated with specific artifacts for South Africans, vulnerability itself is universally a feature of human experience. Recognizing this inescapable dimension of experience leads to appreciating that the struggle against apartheid was not simply a struggle for sovereignty. It was not a struggle to eliminate vulnerability; it was a struggle to manage vulnerability. The distorting ambitions of apartheid to realize a vision of sovereignty in which, as Verwoerd put it, human nature does not become an obstacle to social engineering, encouraged in the rhetoric of the liberation struggle—as exemplified by Robert Sobukwe's challenge to the pass laws— an ambition to acknowledge and express vulnerability more generously. This ambition must not resort to a self-serving claim for authority at the expense of the agency of others. The rhetoric of the struggle must give expression to the possibilities both feared and longed for in the frailty of the human condition.

Continued controversies in democratic South Africa reveal the struggle to acquire a critical vocabulary for reflecting on our capacity to manage our vulnerabilities as we strive to participate to describe the common good that joins us with each other in public life. It is a struggle to develop what James Beitler terms "rhetorics of interdependence." Developing such rhetorics, learning to earnestly engage each other, is not simply a matter of being able to comprehend and describe and enact virtues such as decency or empathy or forgiveness. The South African experience has no doubt much more to teach us about these matters. Feelings for the suffering of others are never untroubled. Every possibility for understanding—whether expressed in words or deeds or monuments or films—requires of people that they engage each other on matters that set them against each other.

For people to successfully come together across their differences in order to create a common good out of their discussions requires they do more than engage in persuading each other of some sense of a good they all can share. The common good they can come to share through their encounters with each other is the product of sharing vulnerabilities about what is feared and what is hoped for. The South African experience in the years since the end of apartheid certainly cautions us about the challenges of such rhetorical vulnerability. More than this, of the many things the South African experience has to teach us, one of the most important is a greater appreciation for the virtues as well as the vices of our vulnerabilities.

WORKS CITED

Adam, Heribert, and Kogila Moodley. *The Opening of the Apartheid Mind: Options for the New South Africa*. Berkeley: University of California Press, 1993.

Alexander, Neville. *An Ordinary Country: Issues in the Transition from Apartheid to Democracy in South Africa*. Pietermaritzburg, South Africa: University of Natal Press, 2002.

Apter, Andrew. *Beyond Words: Discourse and Critical Agency in Africa*. Chicago: University of Chicago Press, 2007.

Arendt, Hannah. *The Human Condition*. Chicago: University of Chicago Press, 1998.

Aristotle. *On Rhetoric*. Trans. George Alexander Kennedy. New York: Oxford University Press, 2007.

Asmal, Kader, Louise Asmal, and Ronald Suresh Roberts. *Reconciliation through Truth: A Reckoning of Apartheid's Criminal Governance*. Cape Town: David Philip Publishers, 1996.

Bacon, Francis. *The Advancement of Learning*. Oxford: Clarendon Press, 1873.

Battle, Michael. *Reconciliation: The Ubuntu Theology of Desmund Tutu*. Cleveland, Ohio: Pilgrim Press, 1997.

Beitler, James Edward III. "Rhetorics of Interdependence: Composing the 'Ethos' of the Greensboro Truth and Reconciliation Commission." Ph.D. diss., University of Michigan, 2009.

Beauregard, Robert A. *Voices of Decline: The Postwar Fate of US Cities*. Cambridge, U.K.: Blackwell, 1993.

Boraine, Alex. *A Country Unmasked: Inside South Africa's Truth and Reconciliation Commission*. Oxford: Oxford University Press, 2000.

Bowker, G. C., and L. Star. *Sorting Things Out: Classification and Its Consequences*. Cambridge, Mass.: MIT Press, 1999.

Bulwer, John. *Chirologia: Or, the Natural Language of the Hand, and Chironomia: Or, the Art of Manual Rhetoric*. Carbondale: Southern Illinois University Press, 1974.

Buntman, Fran Lisa. "The Politics of Conviction: Political Prisoner Resistance on Robben Island, 1962–1991, and its Implications for South African Politics and Resistance Theory." Ph.D. diss. University of Texas at Austin, 1997.

———. *Robben Island and Prisoner Resistance to Apartheid*. Cambridge, U.K.: Cambridge University Press, 2003.

Burke, Kenneth. *Language as Symbolic Action*. Berkeley: University of California Press, 1966.

Chiba, Laloo. Interview with author. Robben Island, October 2000.

Chigwedere, Pride, George R. Seage III, Sofia Gruskin, Tun-Hou Lee, and M. Essex. "Estimating the Lost Benefits of Antiretroviral Drug Use in South Africa." *Journal of Acquired Immune Deficiency Syndrome* 49 (2008): 410–15.

Cockrell, Alfred. "Rainbow Jurisprudence." *South African Journal on Human Rights*. 12.1 (1996): 1–38.

Coombes, Annie E. *Visual Culture and Public Memory in a Democratic South Africa*. Durham, N.C.: Duke University Press, 2003.

Davids, Nashira, and Moipone Malefane. "Tutu to Zuma: 'Watch Out.'" http://www .dispatch.co.za/news/article/2100 (accessed October 19, 2011).

De Gruchy, John W. *Reconciliation: Restoring Justice*. London: SCM Press, 2002.

De Klerk, F. W. *The Last Trek: A New Beginning*. London: Pan Macmillan, 1998.

Deacon, Harriet. "Remembering Tragedy, Constructing Modernity: Robben Island as a National Monument." In *Negotiating the Past: The Making of Memory in South Africa*, ed. Sarah Nuttall and Carli Coetzee. New York: Oxford University Press, 1999, 161–79.

District 9. Dir. Neill Blomkamp, Perf. Sharlto Copley, David James, and Jason Cope. Sony Pictures Home Entertainment, 2009. DVD.

Dlamini, Moses. *Hell-Hole Robben Island: Reminiscences of a Political Prisoner*. Nottingham, U.K.: Spokesman, 1984.

Doxtader, Erik. "Characters in the Middle of Public Life: Consensus, Dissent, and *Ethos*." *Philosophy and Rhetoric* 33 (2000): 336–69.

———. "Making Rhetorical History in a Time of Transition" *Rhetoric & Public Affairs* 4.2 (2001): 223–60.

———. *With Faith in the Works of Words: The Beginnings of Reconciliation in South Africa, 1985–1995*. East Lansing: Michigan State University Press, 2008.

———. "Works of Faith, Faith of the Works: A Reflection on the Truth and Justification of Forgiveness" *Quest* 16.1–2 (2002): 50–60.

Dugard, John. "Retrospective Justice: International Law and the South African Model." In *Transitional Justice and the Rule of Law in New Democracies*, ed. A. James McAdams. Notre Dame, Ind.: University of Notre Dame Press, 2001. 269–91.

English, Rosalind. "Ubuntu: The Quest for an Indigenous Jurisprudence." *South African Journal on Human Rights* 12.4 (1996): 641–48.

Englund, Harri. *Prisoners of Freedom: Human Rights and the African Poor*. Berkeley: University of California Press, 2006.

Fleming, David. "The Space of Argumentation: Urban Design, Civic Discourse, and the Dream of the Good City." *Argumentation* 12 (1998): 147–66.

Forrest, Drew, and Barry Streek. "Mbeki in Bizarre AIDS Outburst." *Mail & Guardian* (Johannesburg). October 26, 2001. http://www.aegis.com/news/dmg/2001/MG011021 .html (accessed October 19, 2011).

"A Freedom Tower for Mandela." July 20, 2005. www.southafrica.info/mandela/freedom statue.htm#longwalk (accessed June 29, 2009).

Fugard, Athol. *The Island*. New York: Viking Press, 1976.

———. *Tsotsi*. New York: Grove Press, 1980.

Galanter, Marc. "Righting Old Wrongs." In Martha Minow, *Breaking the Cycles of Hatred: Memory, Law, and Repair.* Introduced and with commentaries edited by Nancy L. Rosenblum. Princeton, N.J.: Princeton University Press, 2002. 107–31.

Gevisser, Mark. *A Legacy of Liberation: Thabo Mbek and the Future of the South African Dream.* New York: Palgrave, 2009.

"Giant Mandela Statue Planned." *Johannesburg Sunday Times.* October 17, 2002.

Gibson, James L. *Overcoming Apartheid: Can Truth Reconcile a Divided Nation?* New York: Russell Sage Foundation, 2004.

———, and Amanda Gouws. *Overcoming Intolerance in South Africa: Experiments in Democratic Persuasion.* Cambridge, U.K.: Cambridge University Press, 2003.

Giliomee, Herman. *The Afrikaners: Biography of a People.* Charlottesville: University of Virginia Press, 2003.

Gobodo-Madikizela, Pumla. *A Human Being Died That Night: A South African Story of Forgiveness.* New York: Houghton Mifflin, 2003.

Goodman, David. "Cape Town's District Six Rises Again" *The Ford Foundation Report* 28.2 (Spring 1997).

Gready, Paul. "Autobiography and the 'Power of Writing:' Political Prison Writing in the Apartheid Era." *Journal of Southern African Studies* 19.3 (1993): 489–523.

Gutmann, Amy, and Dennis Thompson. *Democracy and Disagreement: Why Moral Conflict Cannot Be Avoided in Politics, and What Should Be Done About It.* Cambridge, Mass.: Harvard University Press, 1996.

Harris, George W. *Dignity and Vulnerability: Strength and Quality of Character.* Berkeley: University of California Press, 1997.

Hatch, John B. *Race and Reconciliation: Redressing Wounds of Injustice.* Lanham, Md.: Lexington Books, 2008.

Howarth, David. "Paradigms Regained? A Critique of Theories and Explanations of Democratic Transition in South Africa." In *South Africa in Transition: New Theoretical Perspectives,* ed. David Howarth and Aletta Norval. New York: St. Martin's Press, 1998. 182–214.

Kathrada, Ahmed. *Letters from Robben Island: A Selection of Ahmed Kathrada's Prison Correspondence, 1964–1989.* Rivonia, South Africa: Zebra Press, 2000.

———. "Opening Address." *EsiQithini: The Robben Island Exhibition.* Cape Town: South African Museum and Bellville, Mayibye Books, 1996.

Katz, Edward and John Rouse. *Unexpected Voices: Theory, Practice, and Identity in the Writing Classroom.* Cresskill, N.J.: Hampton Press, 2003.

Kernberg, Otto. *Aggressivity, Narcissism, and Self-Destructiveness in the Psychotherapeutic Relationship: New Developments in the Psychopathology and Psychotherapy of Severe Personality Disorders.* New Haven, Conn.: Yale UP, 2004.

Klein, Naomi. *The Shock Doctrine: The Rise of Disaster Capitalism.* New York: Henry Holt and Co., 2008.

Korff, Gottfried. "From Brotherly Handshake to Militant Clenched Fist: On Political Metaphors for the Worker's Hand." *International Labor and Working-Class History* 42 (Fall 1992): 70–81.

Krog, Antjie. *Country of My Skull: Guilt, Sorrow, and the Limits of Forgiveness in the New South Africa*. New York: Three Rivers Press, 2000.

Long Night's Journey into Day. Dir. Deborah Hoffmann and Frances Reid. California Newsreel, 2000. DVD.

Mabin, Alan. "Dispossession, Exploitation and Struggle: An Historical Overview of South African Urbanization." *The Apartheid City and Beyond: Urbanization and Social Change in South Africa*. David Smith, ed. New York: Routledge, 1992. 13–24.

Macedo, Stephen, ed. *Deliberative Politics: Essays on Democracy and Disagreement*. New York: Oxford University Press, 1999.

Malan, Rian. *My Traitor's Heart: A South African Exile Returns to Face His Country, His Tribe, and His Conscience*. New York: Grove Press, 1990.

Mamdani, Mahmood. *Citizen and Subject: Contemporary Africa and the Legacy of Late Colonialism*. Princeton, N.J.: Princeton University Press, 1996.

Mandela, Nelson. *Long Walk to Freedom: The Autobiography of Nelson Mandela*. New York: Little, Brown and Co., 1994.

Mansbridge, Jane. "Everyday Talk and the Deliberative System." In *Deliberative Politics*, ed. Macedo. 211–42.

Marback, Richard. "A Meditation on Vulnerability in Rhetoric" *Rhetoric Review* 29.1 (2010): 1–13.

———. "A Tale of Two Plaques: Rhetoric in Cape Town." *Rhetoric Review* 23.3 (2004): 253–68.

———. "The Rhetorical Space of Robben Island." *Rhetoric Society Quarterly* 34.2 (2004): 7–27.

Markell, Patchen. *Bound by Recognition*. Princeton, N.J.: Princeton University Press, 2003.

McCaslin, John. "To Know South Africa: Island Jail of Apartheid Era Open to Tourists." *Washington Times*. January 18, 2003.

McComiskey, Bruce, and Cynthia Ryan, eds. *City Comp: Identities, Spaces, Practices*. Albany: SUNY Press, 2003.

McNeill, David. *Gesture & Thought*. Chicago: University of Chicago Press, 2005.

Merleau-Ponty, Maurice. *Phenomenology of Perception*. Trans. Colin Smith. New York: Routledge, 2003.

Miller, William Ian. *The Anatomy of Disgust*. Cambridge, Mass.: Harvard University Press, 1997.

Minow, Martha. *Between Vengeance and Forgiveness: Facing History after Genocide and Mass Violence*. Boston: Beacon Press, 1998.

Moon, Claire. *Narrating Political Reconciliation: South Africa's Truth and Reconciliation Commission*. New York: Lexington Books, 2009.

Moriarty, Thomas A. *Finding the Words: A Rhetorical History of South Africa's Transition from Apartheid to Democracy*. Westport, Conn.: Praeger, 2003.

Mountford, Roxanne. "On Gender and Rhetorical Space." *RSQ* 30.1 (2001): 41–71.

Mudimbe, V. Y. *The Idea of Africa*. Bloomington: Indiana University Press, 1994.

Mzamane, M. V. "Robben Island: Our University." *Ufahamu* 17.3 (1989): 92–98.

Norval, Aletta J. *Deconstructing Apartheid Discourse*. New York: Verso, 1996.

Nussbaum, Martha. *Upheavals of Thought: The Intelligence of Emotions*. New York: Cambridge University Press, 2001.

Orr, Wendy. *From Biko to Basson: Wendy Orr's Search for the Soul of South Africa as a Commissioner of the TRC*. Saxonwold, South Africa: Contra Press, 2000.

Ottaway, David. *Chained Together: Mandela, de Klerk, and the Struggle to Remake South Africa*. New York: Times Books, 1993.

Paul, Samuel A. *The Ubuntu God: Deconstructing a South African Narrative of Oppression*. Eugene, Ore.: Pickwick Publications, 2009.

Pheko, S. E. M. *The Land Is Ours: The Political Legacy of Mangaliso Sobukwe*. New York: Pheko & Associates, 1994.

Pogrund, Benjamin. *How Can Man Die Better: The Life of Robert Sobukwe*. Jeppestown, South Africa: Jonathan Ball Publishers Ltd., 1997.

———. *Sobukwe and Apartheid*. Johannesburg, South Africa: Jonathan Ball, 1990.

Prophets of da City. "Neva Again." *Universal Souljaz*. Nation, 1995. CD.

"Proposed Memorial Must Remember All Apartheid's Vicitms. Cape Times, April 1, 1996. n.p.

Prosalendis, Sandra, Jennifer Marot, Crain Soudien, and Anwah Nagia. "Punctuations: Periodic Impressions of a Museum." In *Recalling Community in Cape Town: Creating and Curating the District Six Museum*, ed. Ciraj Rassool and Sandra Prosalendis. Cape Town: District Six Museum, 2001. 74–95.

Ramoupi, Neo Lekgotla laga. "Working on Robben Island." http://legacy.matrix.msu.edu/sanch/amagugu2/neo.htm (accessed October 20, 2011).

Republic of South Africa. Parliament. House of Assembly Debates, 3, April 24, 1963, p. 4652.

"Resource Sovereignty: Congo, Africa and the Global South." http://sfbayview.com/2011/nationalize-mines-and-banks-says-south-africa%E2%80%99s-julius-malema/ (accessed October 19, 2011).

Ricouer, Paul. *Oneself as Another*. Chicago: University of Chicago Press, 1992.

Robben Island: Our University. Produced and directed by Lindy Wilson. 1988. 55 minutes.

Rosenfeld, S. *A Revolution in Language*. Palo Alto, Calif.: Stanford University Press, 2001.

Salazar, Philippe-Joseph. *An African Athens: Rhetoric and the Shaping of Democracy in South Africa*. Mahwah, N.J.: Lawrence Erlbaum Associates, 2002.

———, Sanya Osha, Wim van Binsbergen, eds. "Truth in Politics: Rhetorical Approaches to Democratic Deliberation in Africa and Beyond." Special Issue of *Quest: An African Journal of Philosophy* 26.1–2 (2002).

Saul, John S. *The Next Liberation Struggle: Capitalism, Socialism and Democracy in Southern Africa*. Scottsville, South Africa: University of KwaZulu-Natal Press, 2005.

Schneider, Helen, and Didier Fassin. "Denial and Defiance: A Socio-Political Analysis of AIDS in South Africa." *AIDS* 16.4 (2002): 45–51.

Shriver, Donald W. *An Ethic for Enemies: Forgiveness in Politics*. New York: Oxford University Press, 1995.

Simmons, Sherwin. "Hand to the Friend, Fist to the Foe: The Struggle of Signs in the Weimer Republic" *Journal of Design History* 13.4 (2000): 319–39.

Simpson, Graeme. "'Tell No Lies, Claim No Easy Victories': A Brief Evaluation of South Africa's Truth and Reconciliation Commission." In *Commissioning the Past: Understanding South Africa's Truth and Reconciliation Commission,* ed. Deborah Posel and Graeme Simpson. Johannesburg, South Africa: Witwatersrand University Press, 2002. 220–51.

Sparks, Allister. *Tomorrow Is Another Country: The Inside Story of South Africa's Negotiated Settlement.* Johannesburg, South Africa: Jonathan Ball Publishers, 1995.

Tambo, Oliver. "Mandela and Nehru." In *Preparing for Power: Oliver Tambo Speaks.* Compiled by Adelaide Tambo. London: Heinemann, 1987. 193–99.

Thompson, Leonard. *A History of South Africa.* New Haven, Conn.: Yale Nota Bene, 2000.

Tomaselli, Keyan, Arnold Shepperson, and Alum Mpofu. "National Symbols: Cultural Negotiation and Policy Beyond Apartheid" *Communication* 22.1 (1996): 53.

Truth and Reconciliation Commission of South Africa Report. 5 vols. Cape Town: Truth and Reconciliation Commission, 1999.

Tsering, Tender. "Zuma Go's Worse Than Apartheid Regime, says Tutu." http://www .phayul.com/news/article.aspx?id=30118 (accessed October 16, 2011).

Tsotsi. Dir. Gavin Hood, Perf. Presley Chweneyagae, Mothusi Magano, Israel Makoe. Miramax, 2006. DVD.

Turner, Bryan. *Vulnerability and Human Rights.* University Park: Pennsylvania State UP, 2006.

Tutu, Desmond. *No Future without Forgiveness.* New York: Image Books, 2000.

Van Binsbergen, Wim. "Postscript: Aristotle in Africa—Towards a Comparative Africanist Reading of the South African Truth and Reconciliation Commission." *Quest* 16.1–2 (2002): 238–72.

Van der Westhuizen, Christi. *White Power & the Rise and Fall of the National Party.* Cape Town: Zebra Press, 2007.

Walzer, Michael. "Deliberation, and What Else?" In *Deliberative Politics,* ed. Macedo. 58–69.

Wilson, Richard A. *The Politics of Truth and Reconciliation in South Africa: Legitimizing the Post-Apartheid State.* Cambridge, U.K.: Cambridge University Press, 2001.

Young, Iris Marion. "Communication and the Other: Beyond Deliberative Democracy." *Intersecting Voices: Dilemmas of Gender, Political Philosophy, and Policy.* Princeton, N.J.: Princeton University Press, 1997. 60–74.

———. "Justice, Inclusion, and Deliberative Democracy." In *Deliberative Politics,* ed. Macedo. 151–58.

Zapiro. "Urban Handscape." *Mail and Guardian.* 3 April 1996.

Zwelonke, D. W. *Robben Island.* London: Heinemann, 1973.

INDEX

www.ingramcontent.com/pod-product-compliance
Lightning Source LLC
Chambersburg PA
CBHW030308100426
42812CB00002B/621